AFTER RELIGION:
Scientific Spirituality

The Next Stage
of Consciousness

Thomas E. McNamara

7/30/2012

Preface

My teaching career as a psychology professor has taken me to universities in the United States, France, Germany, Egypt and Japan. As I taught students in each of those cultures I became more and more fascinated with the influence of culture on consciousness. When I retired, some ten years ago, I wrote a book on what I had learned.[1] The essential premise of my thesis is that human consciousness is instinctual, but our self-consciousness is learned. This book is an application of this theory of how culture shapes self-consciousness and the essential role of religion in that evoloutuionary process.

The most important evolutionary development in the history of our species has been the gradual emergence of a radically new form of consciousness. The scientific understanding of the human mind has now advanced sufficiently to show that our present form of consciousness—rational self-consciousness— is simply a form of our original, primate consciousness. Seen from a scientific perspective, this normal way of thinking, which every culture inculcates in its members, is inherently defective because it evolved to address the problems of our prehistoric ancestors. It is the mismatch between this ancient form of instinctual consciousness and the modern world that is the root cause of most of the individual and societal problems in the world today. Scientific spirituality allows the human mind to fully integrate all of its needs and desires, which is impossible if we are limited to our normal consciousness. Our species must evolve into this new kind of consciousness if it is ever to reach its full potential for both individualism and a fully functioning form of civilization. This book presents the origin of normal consciousness and explains how it can be transformed in order to release the full potential of the human mind.

AFTER RELIGION:
Scientific Spirituality
The Next Stage of Consciousness

AFTER RELIGION:
Scientific Spirituality

The Next Stage
of Consciousness

By

Thomas E. McNamara

© 2012

I. INTRODUCTION:
CONSCIOUSNESS, CULTURE, AND MEANING

In my first book,[2] I suggested that because of the contributions of Darwin and Mendel, Freud and Heidegger, Einstein and Plank, Skinner and Hebb, Hamilton, Dawkins, and Pinker, there is now emerging a new understanding of human nature. In this book, I will explore contemporary modifications and implications of that model of the mind based on some radically new ideas in theology, such as those of J. D. Crossan, creator of the Jesus Seminar, and in evolutionary biology, such as E. O. Wilson's new theory of the role of group selection in human evolution.[3] Since my own background is in clinical psychology, I will focus on how this new model of human nature reveals some dramatic flaws in our culture and our self-understanding, especially in terms of religion, rationalism, individualism, and our conception of freedom.

The chimps and the bonobos have shown us that primate species are very good at adapting to their environment by creating a culture that best serves their instinctual needs in that particular environment. It is especially instructive to see that even relatively minor differences in natural environments can produce such dramatically different cultural values as the contrast in sexual behavior between these two sibling species, which live on opposite sides of the Zaire River.[4] But now we must harness that force of nature, cultural programming, to create a radically new, fully human culture. Otherwise, our own species will not long endure. This, of course, is a long-term solution; in the meantime, we need to rely on political means to reconstruct our democratic experiment so that it can once again become the beacon of humanistic culture that will motivate all the rest of the human family to emulate our fully human society. The time has come for the thoughtful, progressive community in America to do more than simply promote tolerance and reason. We must construct a fully humanitarian vision for the future of this great nation.

As I proposed in my first book, and as Davidson's recent research demonstrates,[5] we can control the preconscious process by which the human mind creates meaning out of experience. That process was formed from the beginning of our species by our hominin instincts, which means that all our ancestors perceived reality in terms of their own mix of instinctual and learned needs. One of the essential functions of religion has always been to maintain cultural norms that inhibited the individual from exhibiting the most extreme forms of egocentric behavior, such as violence, theft, and rape, because such behaviors threatened social stability. Now psychology has advanced enough to give us the means, as demonstrated by Davidson, to actually alter that instinctual process for the creation of meaning so as to create a society in which no one would want to engage in totally self-centered behavior. A fully human culture would develop our social potential by structuring consciousness in a way that motivates us to identify with each other rather than exploit each other. The mystics, such as Jesus, called this fully human society the "Kingdom of Heaven."

This reframes the question of human freedom in a demonstrably scientific context. Ever since Helmholtz,[6] science has proclaimed that there is no human freedom, as we have seen in the work of Freud and Skinner, for example. Now we have discovered that while it is true that we are determined by our own perception of reality, that perception is itself always subjective. In other words, the conscious mind is preconsciously determined, but the unconscious processes that produce consciousness can be consciously changed. That is the import of Davidson's research, and that discovery is the key to the further evolution of our species.

Symbolic cultures cultivate symbolic realities, by which I mean that their members are programmed to believe that metaphysical values are just as real a motivator as biological needs, such as hunger or fear. This mentality can be seen in Western culture, for example, in the traditional motto of the British military so often invoked before battle: "For God and country." We Americans had to modify that invocation because of our constitutional separation of church and state. So when our political leaders want to motivate us at the deepest level, they employ a cultural, but secular, variation, such as "to defend our American way of life." Every culture has some such core symbolic value that motivates its people so deeply that many of them willingly engage in behavior that threatens their own well-being. Such is the motivational power of symbolic cultures and the way of thinking they inculcate.

Because symbolic thinking (and feeling) plays an essential role in the formation of the self-concept, symbols are the ultimate motivators within the mind itself. So, just as social leaders manipulate symbols to influence behavior at the social level, socially reinforced symbols also motivate at the deepest level of individual consciousness. In the Middle Ages of Western culture, for example, the concept of eternal salvation was a core motivating symbol on both the social and the individual level. In our culture, the symbol we call *money* plays an equally powerful role. Because every ego wants to protect itself by controlling its environment (driven by the deepest of hominin instincts: survival), wealth symbolizes that egocentric need for power and control. As a result, we are all programmed to desire money as an end in itself; that is the essence of materialism, which is a distortion of our own human nature and produces endless harm on both the individual and the social level. Traditional religions often rail against this blatant materialism, yet it continues unabated. This is because religion, which is itself also a product of symbolic consciousness, is actually powerless against our symbolic, egocentric needs.

In order for any religion to guide us back to our undistorted, non-symbolic understanding of our own human nature, it would have to reveal the seeds of its own destruction. The great mystics of the past realized intuitively that such symbolic thinking blocked our ability to perceive ourselves and reality as they are. For the mystic, the true meaning of such religious slogans as "divine revelation" or "absolute truth" is simply one's present experience, in and of itself. People believe they experience their own reality objectively, but the mystics discovered, and now every introduction to psychology textbook explains, that perception itself is learned and the influence of culture plays a fundamental role in that early childhood learning.

This is the human predicament. Our ability to perceive reality has always been warped by the deep, instinctual learning of our childhood, which I call cultural programming. Evolution made such programming a universal part of childhood development because it adapted the individual to function successfully as a member within whatever reproductive group she or he was raised, just as it programs us all for membership in our linguistic environment. Once the self-concept emerges, usually between the ages of five and seven, it becomes the psychological context or filter through which that individual perceives reality for the rest of life. The resulting ego is well adapted to that particular social context and that greatly facilitates survival and reproduction, but the price paid is a permanent distortion of oneself and of one's experience. This distortion inevitably results in conflict within the mind and in the individual's relationships with others, but that is of no importance to evolution because individual happiness or psychological development beyond reproductive success is itself of no importance to evolution.

In terms of the modern world, this distorted development, with its symbolic consciousness, causes widespread problems on both the individual and the social level. The fundamental flaw is that we all try to solve our problems by means of symbolic thinking because we do not realize that such thinking is itself the cause of those problems. For example, two of the most cherished values in contemporary American culture are personal freedom and privacy. These are, of course, perfectly legitimate values, but they can be so easily corrupted by egocentric needs that they often become justifications for egocentrism, thus preventing the further evolution of the common good. Think of the neglected child who grows up to become an antisocial adult, the repeat drunk driver who finally kills somebody, the serial rapist, the financial crook like Bernie Madoff, or the absolute dictator, such as we see in North Korea. We refuse to intervene in such patterns of unhealthy development until the damage is done because of our metaphysical values. We have the means to prevent crime, not just punish it, but we refuse to do so because that would violate our cultural values. We maintain a judicial system, for example, that systematically sacrifices individuals in order to preserve the personal freedoms of the majority. We say that we believe in the transcendent value of each individual, yet we do nothing to protect individuals from predictable victimization because our cultural values program us to believe that our metaphysical values are more important than the individual. Just look at the enormous resistance to even the most innocuous forms of gun control, for example.

In terms of optimal psychological health, it is useful to think of symbolic consciousness as a pandemic spectrum disorder. Everyone suffers from it to some degree, and that degree is determined by how monolithic the cultural value system was in that individual's childhood. People raised in a modern, secular society, such as most Western nations today, are automatically exposed to a diverse mix of values and so are forced to conclude that human experience can be understood in a variety of ways. This serves as a partial inoculation against the most virulent form of egocentrism. Those raised in a strict religious family and community are demonstrably less open to opposing ideas or values. And people raised in religiously and politically monolithic cultures are clearly inhibited in their potential for perceiving reality from "foreign" perspectives. Consider the resistance against the education of women in many traditional religious cultures.

We need scientific morality and politics, which means we must learn to put all of our most cherished beliefs to the test of the scientific method. For example, we continue to legislate morality even though we know from our own history that it is not an effective way to alter human behavior. Abortion, recreational drug use, sexual orientation, extramarital sex (cf. the values of the founders of Western culture, for example), and the role of government—all of these issues can be examined and evaluated in terms of their various outcomes. We must give up judging issues based on culturally ingrained emotions and begin to put them to scientifically valid, empirical tests. Logical thinking is a natural resource that is not natural to our instinctual, symbolic consciousness and so it must be consciously cultivated on the cultural level.

Symbolic consciousness can use logic but only to serve its inherently emotional purposes. For example, we think we are being logical when we believe that we can be domineering, even aggressive, on the job but perfectly kind and loving at home ("Leave your work in your office"). But that is like believing that you can work in a biologically toxic environment all day and yet be perfectly healthy once you walk through your front door at home! Our ability to manipulate symbols to serve our egocentric needs condition us to believe that our psychology and our biology are completely separate and independent dimensions of our lives. This is a denial of basic science that the mystics intuitively realized was nonsense. Life is one.

Only scientific truth can set us free—from being controlled by our own cultural programming. However, such freedom can only be achieved by a process of depression followed by rebuilding motivation based on one's own chosen values. This is a radically new stage of human development, unknown to clinical psychology, which considers depression to be intrinsically dysfunctional. The first law of any culture is to program its members to believe that membership in it is essential to happiness, thus making excommunication a kind of death. This is why Jesus said we must die to ourselves in order to live in the kingdom, as we shall see.

Another radical discovery of how the mind works is that symbolic consciousness makes all emotional needs fungible, such that if your marriage is falling apart, you could be more motivated to seek career success, rather than to address the real issues in the marriage (which would be like putting a bandage on your forehead because you cut your finger). Combine this characteristic with our new understanding of the motivational plasticity of the central nervous system (CNS), and you realize that we are all controlled by our mental environment, even though we ourselves have created that environment in our own acculturation. We are led to the conclusion that we must now turn our attention to our own mental environment, rather than focus on our ability to manipulate our external environment. The "next big thing" should not be just another technological innovation, but a radical change in our own way of perceiving ourselves and our environment. Traditionally, of course, that task has been dominated by culture and religion, so it is there that we must begin the process of societal change.

To make understanding these interrelated theories easier, I have decided to deviate from the standard scientific format of presenting evidence first and concluding with new theories. Instead, this book begins with my theory of religion's prehistoric emergence and the reasons why we must now replace it within the concept of scientific spirituality. Next, I explore what made religion possible in the first place: the evolution of our present form of consciousness. Then I will conclude with the essential characteristics of scientific spirituality.

II. The Evolutionary Function of Religion

In the conclusion of her masterful summary of the origins of all of the world's great religious traditions, Karen Armstrong gives her own conclusions about the nature of true spirituality, which is quite different from any set of theological doctrines:

> Regardless of their theological "beliefs," which, as we have seen, did not much concern the sages—they all concluded that if people made a disciplined effort to reeducate themselves, they would experience an enhancement of their humanity. In one way or another, their programs were designed to eradicate the egotism that is largely responsible for our violence and promoted the empathic spirituality of the Golden Rule. This, they found, introduced people to a different dimension of human experience. It gave them *ekstasis*, a "stepping out" from their habitual, self-bound consciousness that enabled them to apprehend a reality that they called "God," *nibbana*, brahman, atman, or the Way. It was not a question of discovering your belief in "God" first and then living a compassionate life. The practice of disciplined sympathy would itself yield intimations of transcendence.[7]

This book could be considered to be simply an attempt to give a neurological and psychological foundation for Ms. Armstrong's statement.

My theoretical model of the emergence and function of religion in human evolution, however, begins by making a fundamental distinction between religion, which is a biological product of our evolution, and spirituality, which is not a product of biological evolution but simply an optional side effect of our neurological development. Consequently, this book has two fundamental theories: one on the development of our current state of consciousness and the other on the central role religion played in bringing us to this form of consciousness. These theories have led me to conclude that we must now take control of the evolution of our own consciousness by creating a developmental culture that enables us to achieve our full psychological and spiritual potential. As I will explain, all traditional religions are by their very nature *opposed* to promoting true psychological individualism.

The theory begins with the current understanding of how the human nervous system evolved since its inception some two hundred thousand years ago. The central nervous systems (CNS) of all primates include neurological plasticity, reentry circuits, and some form of an altricial period. There is growing evidence that natural selection has dramatically increased these parts in the development of our own CNS. This evidence suggests that these mutations were likely driven by our ancestors' migration out of Africa some one hundred thousand years ago. Placed into radically different environments, they must have faced powerful selective pressure for rapid adaptation. For this reason, natural selection favored biological mutations that improved our plasticity and reentry circuits and also extended our altricial period. In short, we made a giant leap in our instinctual ability to learn—forever morphing us into something more than just another species of hominins.

These radical changes were most manifest in the emergence of grammatical language. Language is what made both symbolic and logical thinking possible, which, in turn, gave rise to self-consciousness. The ability to learn and think symbolically—beginning with language and expanded by religion—emerged as a result of these biological mutations. Consequently, we became faster and more flexible learners than any other species on earth. But it is essential to understand that this enormous increase in learning ability in no way changed our original hominin instincts or desires. Symbolic learning and thinking simply made our basic instincts more fungible, abstract, and conceptual. Those instincts include, of course, our original hominin instincts of sex and survival, but also a deep social instinct, since we hominins are a very social species. We see the influence of this primal instinct especially in our need for a socially defined ego that incorporates the values and attitudes of our family and culture, which was essential to the emergence of religion.

Our modern Western culture has programmed us all to believe that because we are capable of rational, self-conscious thinking, we must be responsible for our decisions. Both our religious and our judicial institutions concur in promulgating this doctrine of personal freedom and responsibility. However, Daniel Kahneman was recently awarded the Nobel Prize for demonstrating that we humans are not rational decision makers most of the time in our daily lives, especially in regard to our economic choices.[8] This challenge to modern rationalism has many other supporters and much empirical evidence within scientific psychology. Michael Gazzaniga, for example, in his prestigious Gifford Lectures, reviewed extensive experimental evidence to show that our conscious mind does not control our behavior. Gazzaniga concedes that our sense of free will is an illusion when he says:

> We accept the fact that our bodies are humming along, being run by automatic systems that follow deterministic laws. Luckily, we don't have to consciously digest our food, keep our heart beating, and our lungs oxygenating. When it comes to our thoughts and actions, however, we don't like to think of those as being nonconscious, following a set of predetermined laws. But the fact remains, and you can show this experimentally, that actions are over, done, kaput, before your brain is conscious of them.[9]

The conscious mind's role is simply to interpret the decisions and feelings of the unconscious mind, *after the fact*, in order to assign meanings that he says make sense to oneself. This is what I mean when I say we all create meanings that are determined by our ego, which is itself a product of our primate instincts, our past environment, and personal experience. It is true that we humans are capable of self-conscious, rational decision making and behavior under ideal conditions. However, that is quite different from stating that we are rational animals, as our cultural heritage would have us believe. It is central to my theory that while we humans are capable of rational decision making, such behavior is not typical or normative. In fact, it is axiomatic among psychologists and psychiatrists that the average individual's reasoning ability is practically powerless against that individual's aroused emotions. Consider, for example, the increasing spread of obesity in the United States, which is clearly the result of self-defeating, irrational behavior on a massive scale.

Because of our self-serving cultural mythology, we think of ourselves as essentially different from other animal species. We like to believe that we are free of the instinctual determinism that is so obvious in the behaviors of other animals. But the social sciences are constantly discovering more evidence that such is not the case, as in the research I just cited. And because we are blind to the fundamental role that our primate emotions play in our daily lives, we also do not fully appreciate the other deep, instinctual predispositions we inherited along with our hominin CNS, such as our need for hierarchy, our need for intra- and interpersonal enforcement of cultural values, and our need for creating egosyntonic meanings of our experiences. We are not normally aware of these needs because they operate on the preconscious level of our mind, beginning in infancy, which is what makes them so powerful. Their influence predisposes us to create certain meanings out of our experiences that are either irrational, not based on empirical evidence, or not the product of logical thinking. Although they permeate every aspect of our daily lives, these irrational characteristics of our nature are most pronounced when it comes to religious thinking. I argue that this irrationality is now the primary threat to our survival as a species.

Our unique human nature, being the product of a random and unintelligent biological process, has many inherent contradictions and is still a work in evolutionary progress. This is because evolution's only objective, in any species, is the survival of the individual organism long enough to reproduce its genetic code. Its purpose has never been the personal well-being or psychological development of the individual organism. One of the primary areas of conflict in our CNS is the tension between our hominin social instincts, best defined by Hamilton's theory of inclusive fitness,[10] and our even deeper fear of death, which manifests itself in our instinctual need for constant defense of our self-symbol, or ego. The original theory of fitness said that it was only the individual's reproductive success that influenced the genetic inheritance of his or her offspring. Hamilton expanded this definition of fitness to include the effects of the individual's behavior on the reproductive success of his or her genetic relatives. This discovery added a social dimension to the process of genetic change and that would by definition include the role of religion and culture.

Religion first emerged within the human community precisely to deal with this conflict by promoting prosocial behaviors, which are driven by our social instinct, and negate our selfish, egocentric survival instinct. Typically fostered in childhood, this prosocial, motivational process begins when a person is taught how to follow the rules of that reproductive community's religious morality. Indoctrinating the child to believe in an imaginary cosmology of gods and devils and, thus, right and wrong behaviors, further reinforces these prosocial, moral behaviors, as does teaching children that "good" behaviors are rewarded and selfish, egocentric ones are punished by an all-powerful god in this life or the next.

III. Symbolic Consciousness Is Still Instinctual Consciousness

As science has shown, what makes our species different is our very prolonged period of instinctual, altricial learning. This initial period in human development is very powerful because of its ability to grow new neurological connections between stored synaptic patterns—a form of plasticity, which enables us to create *any* meaning out of *any* experience. Natural selection favored this new form of learning to control human behavior in much the same way that hominin instincts controlled the behavior of preceding hominin species. The result is that each child is emotionally programmed by her culture with the same values and beliefs that were successful for the preceding generations of that reproductive community. This evolutionary adaptation—a consciousness based on instinctual social learning—is the origin of our unconscious emotional need to perceive reality through a lens shaped by our socially imposed childhood worldview, rather than the full complexity of our actual environment, with its continuous process of change across an almost infinite composite of variables.

Leon Festinger's theory of cognitive dissonance, which proposes that we have an innate desire to resolve conflicts between our behavior and our attitudes, was an early indication of the mind's bias toward integration of beliefs and behavior. Recently, Michael Shermer has extended this developmental characteristic of our species with his theory of belief-dependent realism, which says that we are preconsciously disposed to perceive reality only in ways that are compatible with our already accepted beliefs. As he put it, "Our perceptions about reality are dependent on the beliefs that we hold about it. Reality exists independent of human minds, but our understanding of it depends upon the beliefs we hold at any given time."[11] This is another example of the power of acculturation. Once we are given a belief by our culture, we tend to "find" evidence for that belief in our ordinary daily perceptions of reality. A baby is discovered alive days after a devastating earthquake and many people perceive that fact as proof of divine intervention in history (i.e., a "miracle"), yet they refuse to make a rational judgment regarding the earthquake itself.

We call our new form of consciousness "self-consciousness," because the self, or ego, is the central, master symbol that provides the context for creating cognitive and emotive meaning out of every experience. Because our creation of meaning is preconscious, we experience the meanings that we are actually creating every day as if they are inherent in the reality of our everyday experiences, even though they are not. Different cultures create different meanings out of similar experiences, just as the same individual often creates different meanings, on different occasions, from the same experience, all the while believing that these created meanings are self-evidently true at that time.

Our symbolic consciousness is the product of the instinctual acquisition of language and culture, usually in childhood, and manifested especially through religion. This is one of the essential changes that resulted from our species' extended altricial period: it is a period of instinctual learning that actually wires both cognitive and emotive circuits in the brain. This deep instinctual learning was selected for because it neurologically programmed the child's CNS to copy the successful values and behaviors that the local culture transmitted to each new member. This radical change in our cognitive and emotive development was essential for our survival when we migrated into radically different natural environments beyond our original home in Africa.

The evolution of consciousness is driven by the first law of evolution: adapt to environmental changes or face extinction. This is why symbolic consciousness emerged and why it changed again as our symbolic thinking helped create another radically new environment: civilization. The creation of civilization has brought us to our current stage of symbolic consciousness, which I will refer to as "egocentric consciousness." People in modern, industrialized cultures like to think of themselves as rational and scientific, but I am proposing that egocentric consciousness is every bit as instinctually driven as our original hominin consciousness of hunting and gathering. In other words, we still create meaning based on our instinctual needs. The only practical difference is that now we incorporate those instinctual needs into our self-concept, which is itself learned instinctually. The best demonstration of this fundamentally instinctual way of thinking is religious belief; by its own definition, "belief" is a commitment to the existence of something that cannot be verified by direct experience. This way of thinking necessarily teaches the child to believe that her own experience is intrinsically secondary to the ideas of the culture. Thus, the real, evolutionary purpose of religion is not the well-being of the individual member, but the control of the individual, inducing each person to conform to the aggregate, successful behaviors of the preceding generations of that reproductive community.

The religious doctrine of original sin, for example, requires believing in a particular theory of human nature that cannot be empirically verified. This doctrine, which is found in some form in every traditional culture and religion, is essential to community control of the individual because it justifies teaching children that they are incapable of creating correct meanings out of their own experiences. Every culture and religion conditions its children to create its cultural meanings out of their own experience or else endure punishment in this life or the next. As a result, children learn to wire synaptic circuits so as to experience the world in the ways their culture and family expects. The best example of this is seen in how we all create our own self-concept—our personal identity—in the first three or four years of life. As Charles Cooley pointed out at the beginning of the twentieth century, we learn to think of ourselves not based on our own experience of ourselves but on what others tell us about ourselves, even when that feedback is inaccurate or unhealthy or both. Herein lies the immense power of the cultural and religious programming of childhood.[12]

IV. Psychology Must
Replace Religion

I am proposing a theory that scientifically explains *how* and *why* egocentric consciousness and religion have been selected for in the evolution of our species. In terms of the psychology of human evolution, I believe that egocentric consciousness and the way of creating meaning out of experience that it engenders are *byproducts* of language acquisition. I will show that this religious mentality, while essential to our evolutionary success one hundred thousand years ago, is now impeding further human development. When we separate consciousness from its religious origins, we see that consciousness is a *natural resource*, like our locking knee or our opposing thumb, and that religious thinking is simply one way of utilizing that resource. Now that we have developed a scientific model of the human mind, we can see that our instinctual consciousness, which is a product of our original hominin culture, is preventing us from developing to our full potential, both individually and socially.

Psychology as a modern science began in the middle of the nineteenth century when Hermann von Helmholtz first measured nerve impulses traveling through the human nervous system. Discovering the electrical nature of the nervous system inspired Helmholtz to propose that the human mind was nothing more than the product of the brain. He concluded that mental activity or self-consciousness required no invoking of any supernatural power or essence. More than 150 years later, psychological research has compiled overwhelming evidence that all functions of the mind, including

11

consciousness itself, are governed by the same laws of nature that determine all other aspects of the known universe. The Helmholtz School of Scientific Physiology became the bedrock of scientific psychology and included such members as Sigmund Freud, Wilhelm Wundt, and B. F. Skinner. In the second half of the twentieth century, evolutionary biology produced additional theoretical support for biological determinism, based on work by such thinkers as William Hamilton, E. O. Wilson, and Richard Dawkins. A new generation of scientists, including Joseph LeDoux, Antonio Damasio, Walter Freeman, and Michael Gazzaniga, are now mapping the actual neurological circuits and physiological mechanisms of our mental life, and, in the process, empirically verifying Helmholtz's model of the mind as a product of nature alone.

Following in that tradition, the theoretical model I propose explicitly denies the very possibility of human freedom and flies in the face of religion, especially the Judeo-Christian tradition of Western culture. If human beings are nothing more than smart animals with thoughts and behaviors determined by the laws of nature, then there is no possibility of personal freedom or responsibility for behavior. Thus, the very moral and judicial foundations of Western civilization are false. The traditions of science and religion are proposing fundamentally different and antithetical theories of human nature. The usual resolution of this conflict, suggested by so many scholars, including the late Stephen Gould, is that science and religion represent two distinct dimensions of human knowledge and, therefore, need not always agree. This suggestion, however, is intellectually untenable, as already established by E. O. Wilson, among others.[13]

It is time for the scientific community to take a stand regarding our cultural and religious understanding of human nature and the nature of religion. Recent years have seen a strong revival of the role of fundamentalist religions in governments, both at home and abroad. This, in turn, has caused a renewed assault on traditional religions in the works of such thinkers as Sam Harris, Daniel Dennett, and Richard Dawkins, who critique their subject on the basis of empirical evidence and logical thinking. Yet the majority of the American people and many others throughout the world continue to declare their faith in religious doctrines and beliefs, knowing full well they are not based on empirical or logical foundations. As mentioned earlier, Michael Shermer has taken a stand by proposing a cogent explanation for this fact in his recent book, *The Believing Brain*, which supports my model of altricial programming and states that "beliefs come first, explanations for beliefs follow."[14]

The growing conflict between faith and reason has the potential to do immeasurable damage to our world and is a conflict that cannot be resolved politically. Democratic governments, by their very nature, cannot determine whether religion is true or false, but religious conflict can, and historically has, destroyed democratic governments. The branch of science best equipped to address this issue is scientific psychology. Following in the footsteps of thinkers like Julian Jaynes, Merlin Donald, Pascal Boyer, and Barbara King, I believe the time has come to take control of our own consciousness and create a developmentally full human culture that will not try to control human behavior but, instead, free it to accept reality as it is and then change the world according to rational principles that are supported by valid scientific evidence.

V. The Dialectic Relationship between Culture and Consciousness

The history of life on earth is replete with a recurring pattern. Every successful new species increases and multiplies in its environment until it reaches a population level that is in balance with the resources available within that particular ecological niche. Our species is no different. At the beginning of hominin evolution in Africa, some six million years before the emergence of our own species, learning produced culture, which then shaped adaptive behaviors within each local reproductive community and transmitted that collective wisdom to each new generation of that community. The power of this new form of adaptation, called acculturation, was so great our hominin ancestors eventually increased their local populations so much that new selective pressures were generated. Recurring population growth at the tribal level must have repeatedly outstripped the capacity of the tribal territory to sustain population growth and, thus, caused natural selection to accelerate and evolve even more successful mutations in the CNS (cf. the Baldwin effect).

We know that several other hominin species evolved and spread out of Africa, probably driven outward because of hunger, long before our own species emerged. So it is reasonable to believe that as our hominin ancestors increased and multiplied, they competed for the same territories and resources with groups of preceding hominin species. We also know that our own species left Africa one hundred thousand years ago and was the sole surviving hominin species some seventy thousand years later. The most likely explanation is that the inevitable intra-hominin competition for territorial resources forced *Homo sapiens* to develop competitive advantages sufficient to win survival. As a result of the competitive stress of this recurring population crisis, the process of natural selection accelerated and produced a brain capable of grammatical language, self-consciousness, and prodigious learning, including motivational learning. It is important to note that, contrary to our own cultural beliefs, none of these changes required anything essentially new in our genome, only alterations in the development of various aspects and stages of the existing hominin genome.

Hamilton's theory of inclusive fitness, as we have seen, shows that altruism, which most people think of as uniquely human, has a genetic basis and is found in many animal species. I argue that hominin acculturation greatly increased at this time in our evolution because it had the effect of extending the genetically based, prosocial attitudes of kinship into the realm of experiential learning. Human acculturation, in the form of religion, automatically implanted in children a spirit of mutual cooperation and trust simply on the basis of shared religious behaviors and values, even if those children were not genetically related. Before the evolution of this advanced form of acculturation, the size of the tribe was essentially limited to the extended family. By means of religious acculturation, however, tribes were able to transcend that biological limitation and increase membership psychologically, rather than biologically, thus making them significantly larger and stronger competitive groups. This evolutionary advantage was so great that it more than compensated for its biological cost—it required *Homo sapiens* to have the longest altricial period by far of any species on earth. This extended form of acculturation still plays such a major role in human life, both on the individual and group level, that it should be considered a hallmark of our species. It is a much greater determinant of our behavior than self-consciousness ever could be, as I will explain.

As a result of this expanded form of adaptation, tribes acculturated in religious thinking increased their populations beyond the size of nonreligious tribes, which were essentially extended families and, thus, won the competition for scarce resources over their neighbors. We may never know the exact neurological details of this genetic change in the CNS, but the end result is clear: the human CNS eventually became capable of high-speed learning, grammatical language, and motivation driven as much by learning as by instinct.

Given these changes, we can explain the most salient aspects of the human mind as it exists today. For example, learning any language means learning symbols; spoken words are simply verbal symbols of the experiences they represent. In addition, once one set of symbols and the rules that govern their manipulation are learned, the CNS is wired to learn additional symbol sets. Numbers in mathematics are simply a particular set of symbols manipulated according to a specific kind of grammar, defined by operations, such as addition, subtraction, division, and multiplication. In other words, mathematics is simply another form of language, as are music, engineering, medicine, and law. The culture of civilization itself, including self-consciousness, is simply the sum total of these various languages.

The CNS's symbolic potential for developing egocentric self-consciousness is also learned from language, even though it did not become psychologically dominant until the rise of civilization. It is simply the result of learning to think of oneself symbolically, in the third person instead of the first person. Gerald Edelman, the Nobel Prize–winning neuroscientist, together with Giulio Tononi, has proposed a neurological theory to explain how self-consciousness evolved. They call this theory "the remembered present," based on the neurological evolution of what they call "re-entry circuits."[15] These circuits function by recirculating synaptic patterns that already exist in the brain together with patterns flowing in from the peripheral nervous system. This recycling process is preconscious and is similar in many ways to the process by which we preconsciously integrate the different synaptic patterns flowing in from our two eyes into a single perceptual field in consciousness. The result of this neurological architecture is that the human mind has the ability to "step out of the present" and imagine having a different experience from the one it is actually having. So, as a result of language acquisition and reentry circuits, we are the only animals who can imagine having an experience that is different from the one that we are actually having. We are the only animals who can imagine something not directly experienced and ask ourselves, "What if?"

There is another, equally important consequence of our unique "reentry consciousness." Pascal Boyer, in his important book on the evolution of religion, *Religion Explained*, makes a very strong case for the importance of inference systems in the preconscious mind.[16] These systems are the unconscious learning that all human beings have formed about all of the important objects and events in their experience. For example, when we look at a photo of our family, we see not only images of individuals in particular poses, but we also preconsciously integrate a host of characteristics of each family member, such as height, voice, and personality. We are not consciously remembering each one of those attributes when we see the images. However, our whole emotional response to the photo is based on the sum total of past learning. We automatically infer from one sensory stimulus a whole set of related, but unconscious, stimuli already stored in our brain, which then play an essential role in shaping our immediate, spontaneous response to that one conscious stimulus.

If we combine Boyer's application of inference theory, which is a contribution from cognitive psychology, with Edelman and Tononi's neurological theory of reentry circuits and the symbolic thinking that we unconsciously learned with our native language, we have a comprehensive, scientific basis for understanding the nature of self-consciousness. Furthermore, this model of self-consciousness also explains why our original self-concept is always composed of what we have been told by others, rather than our own direct experience of our personality and reality, as Cooley pointed out long ago. Just as we use unconscious inferences about others when we interact with them, we have also learned inferences about ourselves from others important to us, which are always active when we think about ourselves. Consequently, such preconscious emotive and cognitive processes play an essential role in shaping our own self-concept and thus shaping our responses (i.e., the meanings) we experience in our daily lives.

Neurological architecture, with its constant mixture of present and past synaptic patterns, ensures that we will always create meaning out of the present based on the past. Our own self-concept is the foundation of the meanings that we create every day because it is the most emotionally powerful manifestation of our original, early childhood social life. Our self-concept is our master symbol because it is the emotional and cognitive bridge between our environment and ourselves. It is the preconscious context out of which we preconsciously create meaning.

VI. Symbols as Motivators

Behavior is evolution's core, so symbols would be of little evolutionary importance if they lacked the power to motivate and shape it. Our learned neurological links between the synaptic patterns we call symbols and our emotional centers are even more important than the cognitive aspect of the mind because they are the source of learned motivation. For example, we know there is a degree of neurological plasticity required in the neocortex that enables the synaptic pattern of the sound of a word to become neurologically linked to the synaptic pattern for the image of the object it represents. Likewise, there must be a similar plasticity in the limbic system that enables the child to grow a neurological connection between a particular emotional response and a particular stimulus. The ability to learn to connect separate synaptic patterns stored in different parts of the brain, and simultaneously to connect to particular emotional centers in the brain, is what makes us so different from other animals. It is this ability that extends our range of responses beyond the purely instinctual range of the hominin. This neurological linking is the biological essence of symbols, without which language, self-consciousness, and personal identity are not possible.

Jean Piaget first showed the existence of this uniquely human plasticity when he demonstrated the difference between what he called the "preoperational" stage of cognitive development and the "formal operational" stage. The preoperational child, between the ages of two and seven years old, can learn symbolic language, but the child is not yet neurologically capable of being motivated by ideas as much as by primate instincts. However, by the age of thirteen, she is capable of violating her hominin instincts because she can now be motivated by learning even more than instinct. This is why teenagers can commit suicide, but five-year-olds cannot. Add to this model Vygotsky's social development theory of learning,[17] and we arrive at a comprehensively biological explanation of human intelligence, underscoring that there exists no essential difference between animal intelligence, artificial intelligence, and our own variety. Just as Hamilton added a social dimension to our understanding of evolution, Vygotsky expanded the classic Piagetian theory of learning by demonstrating the crucial role of social interaction in cognitive development.

As Donald Hebb first discovered[18] and as Merlin Donald[19] and Richard Shweder[20] have proposed, in terms of cultural acquisition, the mind is literally shaped by its earliest childhood environment. Albert Bandura's social-cognitive theory of socialization[21] also states that brain circuits are determined by experience. But the best example comes from research on language acquisition. Saffran and Thiesen have clearly shown that children learn their native language by preconscious statistical analysis.[22] Hebb's rule helps explain that the more often a child hears the same word spoken, the stronger the memory or stored synaptic pattern of that word becomes in the brain. Simply put, Hebb showed that neurons that fire together, wire together. So, the child's brain automatically links the sound of that word with the stimulus that is present at the time of learning. And the same process also accounts for the acquisition of grammar and syntax. The only change is that different circuits are being programmed. Neurological circuits that are stimulated by the environment are strengthened, while synaptic connections that are not stimulated disappear from the CNS—Again, neurons that fire together, wire together, and vice versa. In other words, our minds literally grow into our early social environment, a neurological process summarized in the popular developmental theory known as "blooming and pruning." The preeminent example of this formative developmental process of the mind, which I refer to as programming, is the involuntary, instinctual acquisition of grammatical language.

I am proposing that this same process of adaptation applies to our instinctual acquisition of cultural values and religion, just as it does to language. The precognitive mental process by which all human beings unconsciously process synaptic patterns to create meaning out of experience is a learned process that is implanted in the neurological circuits of the child by learning language and culture. Given this understanding of acculturation, the conclusion is that culture plays a vastly more powerful role in human life than previously thought. And embedded in the core of every traditional culture is some form of religion because that way of thinking played a vital role in the evolution of our species.

Childhood acculturation wires the brain, beginning with social relationships and with language, so as to produce thinking that conforms to the cultural and religious norms of that social environment. Self-consciousness is a side effect of language acquisition because it teaches us how to think about ourselves in essentially the same way we think about others—linguistically, or within the bounds of our language system. As such, self-consciousness is a learned way of thinking and a form of consciousness that requires us to form a self-concept. As we have seen, that concept is simply an aggregate symbol of the sum total of synaptic patterns that we have been told about ourselves by important others. This explains the curious fact that while we all learned about our physical environment by direct experience, we learned about ourselves and formed our self-concept not from our own experience of ourselves but from other people. We all learned about gravity by falling down, a direct experience, just as we learned how to stand up and walk and ride a bicycle. However, we all learned to define ourselves primarily in terms of what was communicated to us by others, not by our own direct experience of our own talents and preferences.

This disparity exists because the circuits of the brain we inherited to learn about the physical environment are remnants of our primate ancestors. The self-concept, on the other hand, is shaped in the memory centers of our language circuits, which are separate and much newer than our primate neurology. Self-consciousness is a mechanism implanted in our mind by learning language, which is part of the new instinctual learning that we call acculturation. And once we learn to think of ourselves in those terms, we are thereby programmed to feel and act accordingly. Evolution favored the religious acculturation development process because it ensured that the collective knowledge of the reproductive community would automatically shape the behavior of the next generation. The development of grammatical language, and the self-consciousness that it generates, represented a major advance in adaptation, which was critical to our evolutionary success.

VII. The Creation of Meaning

I suggest that this instinctual, yet learned, way of creating meaning out of experience guarantees that we will always create meaning out of present sensory patterns based on our past learning. This way of thinking is, after all, what we usually refer to as the most basic form of learning. It is also the normal way that all animals learn, as Pavlov's dogs taught us so well. When we learned to read, for example, we learned to interpret the meaning of a present visual synaptic pattern by linking it in our mind to a remembered auditory synaptic pattern. We accomplished this by sounding out the letters of the written word until the sounds of the letters reminded us of the already learned sound of that word. But once that synaptic connection was made in the association cortex of the brain, we needed only to see the word to instantly hear its sound and remember its associations, which constitute its meaning. This is Hebb's rule at work. As such, the meaning of the present visual stimulus now comes from its neurological linkage to our stored synaptic pattern for the sound of that word. Learning means creating meaning out of the present (stimulus) based on the past (stored synaptic pattern in the association cortex).

I propose that this way of preconsciously creating meaning out of the related synaptic patterns of past experience, combined with symbolic associations, was the essential development that made both religion and civilization possible. We usually think of religion in terms of beliefs, but I am positing that the essence of religion is this particular way of creating meaning out of experience. This new form of consciousness, egocentric consciousness, being a by-product of language acquisition, is a way of *thinking* that no one person could have simply invented. It evolved by natural selection and then was automatically transmitted to each child through acculturation.

Egocentric consciousness, which is the product of the combination of linguistically induced symbolic associations, necessarily results in this instinctual way of creating meaning out of experience. This new form of consciousness evolved because it gave us victory over our hominin rivals by enabling us to learn from each other's experience, to form larger tribes, to develop more complex behaviors and relationships, and to pass on this unique learning to future generations. But the motivational drives of egocentric consciousness in humans are essentially the same as those of all other hominins.

This neurological expansion of learning to include instinctual motivation, together with grammatical language, was essential to our success as a species. Other mammalian species are capable of learning, but no other has the capacity to be as strongly motivated by learning as by biological instincts. We are the only species for whom learning, beginning with religion, has become just as powerful an instinct as sex or survival. In other words, we evolved sufficiently enlarged neocortex learning capacity such that the experientially driven reentry circuits of the frontal lobes developed synaptic connections to the motor centers equal to the instinctually driven circuits of the limbic system. This neurological change was accomplished by making stored synaptic patterns, i.e., past experience, just as strongly connected to the emotional centers of the limbic system as our instincts, which is a unique neurological development in the history of life on earth.

In the beginning of our own species, our original, genetically based tribal communities were defined by the very same hominin instinctual values and behaviors as their predecessors. *Homo sapiens* were just as driven by hominin instinct to: 1) live in hierarchies (an adaptation for coping with scarcity), 2) obey the territorial imperative (for protecting food sources), and 3) practice genetically based altruism (to increase genetic replication) as our hominin rivals. In our beginning, these evolutionary changes in our genetic code simply reflected extensions of CNS trends that were already evident in the six-million-year evolution of the hominin line, yet they resulted in dramatic psychological changes.

Even though these neurological changes gave us the capacity for dramatically more advanced adaptations, those advances could not have emerged unless driven by some crisis between our environment and ourselves. So, in the very beginning, our species was probably no different in lifestyle and consciousness from the already established hominin species, such as the Neanderthal. We are simply the latest in a line of hominin species that was characterized from the beginning by the ability to discover adaptive behaviors by trial and error and to transmit those new behaviors to the next generation by acculturation. Despite this enormous potential for learning, which was equal to the power of instinct in determining behavior, our behaviors were the same as previous hominins because we lived in essentially the same natural and social environment.

Egocentric consciousness is inherently conservative. It was selected for precisely because it ensured the consistent transmission of the collective learning of preceding generations (i.e., culture), while only allowing basic changes when they were required for survival or reproductive success. Therefore, I suggest that even though symbolic thinking first emerged one hundred thousand years ago, it failed to produce significant changes in our hominin culture until some fifty thousand years ago. Here, I am referencing the period in prehistory that Jared Diamond[23] and others have called "the great leap forward," when the rate of cultural change increased dramatically, especially with the emergence of new tools and social customs.

As we have seen, the emergence of grammatical language gave us the CNS potential to generate self-consciousness and the self-symbol or ego. But the culture of egocentric consciousness inhibited this potential because all cultures resist innovation not directly driven by our biological, hominin instincts. Eventually, however, as our ancestors' reproductive communities became larger and more stable in their new environments outside Africa, the demands of adaptation to increasingly complex social environments modified our symbolic consciousness into individualized, egocentric consciousness. This adaptation's first manifestation, along with grammatical language, was probably the emergence of ancestor worship, which slowly evolved into organized religious rituals and symbols.

VIII. Religion Combines Learned Symbols with Instinctual Motivation

The essential evolutionary advantage of religious consciousness was its motivational power, which was achieved neurologically by linking the instinctual centers of fear and desire with the learned values and attitudes of religion, thereby shaping behavior. This crucial set of adaptations only required neurological changes in the CNS that enlarged memory capacity and the neurological pathways between the fear centers (such as the amygdala), the desire centers (such as the nucleus accumbens), and the learning centers of the neocortex (such as the hippocampus). The result allowed symbolic thinking to become a new form of learned motivation that made possible such human abilities as delayed gratification and the intentional division of labor.

Our culture tells us that we first decide on the meaning of an experience and then respond to the experience based on that meaning. However, we know that two people can create very different meanings from the same experience. Consider two people riding together on a roller coaster. One could find the experience delightful, while the other could find it frightening. Freud explained this common phenomenon by showing that childhood experience shapes the adult personality and that personality is the source of all the meanings we humans ascribe to our daily lives. It is interesting to note that this conclusion put Freud in agreement with the theologian Thomas Aquinas, who was the first Western thinker to proclaim that meaning exists only in the human mind, not in nature.

Now, neuropsychology is verifying this basic insight by showing that the essence of every personality is physically located in the neurological circuits of the CNS and those synaptic pathways were primarily formed by social experience (i.e., instinctual learning) during the altricial period of childhood. This is why children who are loved and cherished grow CNS pathways that have neurological links to positive emotional centers in the limbic system and, thus, they can create positive meanings out of normal, healthy experiences. But children who are rejected or abused often grow pathways to the emotional centers of fear and insecurity. As a result, they create meanings later in life that are essentially negative and often filled with anger, aptly summarized in the clinical aphorism: "Hurt people hurt people."

Accordingly, I suggest that children raised in traditional religious cultures grow pathways that lead them to be afraid if they violate their received cultural values and to feel good when they obey. Religions that formed such pathways were favored by evolution because they ensured that members would normally conform to the collective standards of the community and—most important—the resulting behaviors would increase the probability of cultural transmission to each new generation, resulting in social stability, cooperation, and successful child rearing within that society.

Thus, the rise of egocentric consciousness, with its combination of symbolic thinking and learned emotional associations, laid the foundation for the gradual development of civilization and our present form of culture. As tribal communities grew larger and more socially complex, their religions evolved into totemic, polytheistic, and then monotheistic mythologies but always functioned to shape individual behaviors that favored the essential cultural values of survival and reproduction, the sine qua non of all evolutionary adaptations. Thus, this neurological process of deriving the meaning of an experience not from empirical evidence but from association with learned symbols became the basis of religious faith. Other animals are not capable of grammatical language or motivational learning, so neither can they engage in symbolic thinking, self-consciousness, or religious motivation. They can only respond to stimuli on the basis of their previous experience of that stimulus or one similar to it. Only we are capable of responding to an empirical stimulus on the basis of symbolic learning, rather than direct, present experience.

We have broken free of our original environment and have achieved the unlimited ability—through imagination—to change our environment intentionally. This ability was selected for because it constitutes one of the greatest advances in evolutionary adaptation in the history of life on earth. Because other animals are unable to escape from the current sensory stimulation provided by their environment, they are unable to change it. Because our reentry circuits enable us to imagine a present situation different from the one we are actually experiencing, we are motivated to change our environment. It is this ability, first manifested in the form of egocentric consciousness, that has made civilization possible. This is the psychology of religious faith, and faith has motivated our species to the most noble, as well as the most bestial, of behaviors.

IX. The Meaning of Spirituality

We find the first historical indications of the emergence of this new form of consciousness some five thousand years ago in the Hindu scriptures of India. As evidenced by the Vedic literature, a few individuals actually achieved, by trial and error, a new form of consciousness but had no way of understanding or communicating this new way of thinking, except through religious terms. The best extant examples of this non-instinctual, and therefore nonreligious, way of creating meaning out of experience can be found in the famous koans of Zen Buddhism, such as the question about the sound of one hand clapping. These original pioneers in the exploration of consciousness have traditionally been called religious mystics simply by default. I am proposing that they were not religious at all. In fact, they were actually opposed to religious consciousness, since all religions are essentially instinctual, and so are the meanings that they indoctrinate. What these mystics personally experienced and tried to teach was a radically new way of creating meaning out of experience. I am proposing that this definition of spirituality, of which both mysticism and the scientific method itself are examples, are simply two manifestations of the same form of non-instinctual consciousness, which I call scientific spirituality.

As I proposed in my first book, this is the conclusion we should draw from the work of many modern experts on the subject of religion and mysticism, such as Carl Jung, Gordon Allport, Abraham Maslow, Alan Watts, Erich Fromm, and Victor Frankl.[24] Furthermore, I propose that the essence of mysticism, as taught by all the world's great spiritual leaders, is the first noninstinctual form of consciousness that uses direct, immediate experience as the primary context for the creation of meaning from experience. The closest that the traditional terminology of spirituality has come to identifying this new way of thinking has been called present-centered consciousness, but it has never had a scientific definition. What tradition has called mysticism can be defined scientifically, I believe, as the psychological process of creating the most satisfying meaning in response to present experience, without the contamination of meaning that egocentric consciousness—through the mode of religious consciousness—requires.

This new way of creating meaning out of experience is the first form of the next stage of human evolution. Civilized, egocentric consciousness was an adaptation to a social environment that required specialized knowledge and functions within the increasingly complex social structures of the human community. As we have seen, egocentric self-consciousness, which is the basis of all forms of religion, is simply a more advanced form of our original, instinctual, and symbolic hominin consciousness.

What tradition refers to as mystical experience, which is the essence of all the great "religious" teachers of history, including all of the founders of the major religions, was the first form of consciousness that was liberated from its instinctual roots. Unfortunately, the teachings of the mystics across times and cultures were inevitably misunderstood by their followers because of the limits of their own normal, egocentric consciousness. Because of the nature of language, mystics were never able to directly communicate their own form of consciousness to their listeners. This problem in communication is analogous to attempting to verbally give a deaf person the experience of Beethoven's *Ninth Symphony*. Language can never replace direct experience—it can only remind the listener of some form of her or his previous experience. Because most, if not all, of any mystic's followers had never had a mystical experience of their own, they lacked the ability to understand the true nature of what the mystic was attempting to teach. So they did the best they could: they interpreted their teacher's statements in terms of their own egocentric consciousness. The result was not mysticism at all, but simply another variety of religion, and thus just another form of instinctual consciousness.

In other words, the followers of any mystic had to create meanings that reflected the instinctual values of their own egocentric, i.e., instinctual, self-consciousness. Because mystical experience, by its very nature, transcends both instinct and conceptualization, the essence of spirituality can never be transmitted verbally or symbolically. For this reason, the spiritual tradition of every culture—which is, at its core, on the same spiritual plane in every cultural context—was inevitably reduced to just another instrument of that particular instinctual culture. Mysticism was transformed by the religious consciousness of the majority of its followers to be just another way the individual is psychologically suppressed because that is the evolutionary function of all cultural programming. Because egocentric consciousness is inherently instinctual, it reduces mystical teachings to instinctual values, such as the literal interpretation of scriptures, literal belief in such spiritual symbols as heaven and hell as physical realities, the belief that good and evil are not symbols of cultural values but categories of absolute truth. The mystics understood that there are no good or bad people. Good and bad, right and wrong, are simply relative terms for labeling conflicting tendencies within the human mind. All those Hollywood movies we love to watch in which the good guy struggles to overcome the bad guys are simply symbols, and reinforcers, of our own cultural programming. We love them because they reaffirm our own desire to believe that our values are better than anyone else's because we are the good guys and anyone who disagrees with us is the bad guy. Most of what any culture calls entertainment is simply some literal form of such reaffirmation of childhood programming. (Art, on the other hand, deals with the very real conflicts that so often occur within the human mind itself.)

A careful analysis of the writings of all the great mystics, including Jesus, reveals that the mystic is anyone who has discovered a new, "present-centered" way of creating meaning out of experience. As my theory proposes, members of all traditional religions who have not achieved mystical experience, create meaning by interpreting all of their immediate experience in terms of their self-concept. To put it in the terms of current neurological research, instinctual consciousness preconsciously imposes past meanings on present experience by processing incoming synaptic patterns through already established limbic and neocortex pathways.

Mystics, however, independently discovered a radically different way of creating meaning out of experience—which is why they are so rare in human history. The essence of mysticism is the acceptance of present experience as an end in itself, to which past learning may then be consciously applied. Mystics do not judge the present in relation to the past because for them every experience is accepted exactly as it is experienced, in and of itself. Another radical difference between mysticism and religion is that mystics are not motivated by fear, while fear is the primary motivator of instinctual, and thus, religious, consciousness. The essence of mystical consciousness is the unconditional acceptance of present experience, while the essence of traditional religious, egocentric consciousness is judging one's present, in terms of one's self-concept. (The spiritual meaning of the phrase "it is what it is" is precisely that. Each experience should be accepted in and of itself—without measuring it and judging it in terms of any metaphysical or emotional norms.)

This new way of creating meaning from experience, having begun with the first mystics more than five thousand years ago, has slowly spread through history and culture, eventually producing most of the major social developments we define as hallmarks of progress, including the scientific movement. I believe that only now, because of the advances of scientific psychology, can we begin to understand spiritual consciousness, which is the next stage in the evolution of human consciousness. Physical behavior is the currency of evolution; consciousness is not. But all human behavior begins in the preconscious processes of the CNS.

Mystical consciousness radically changes those preconscious processes and thereby fundamentally changes human behavior. Egocentric consciousness, of which religion is the primordial manifestation, drives behavior on the basis of the individual's instinctual fears and desires. Present-centered consciousness, the essence of scientific spirituality, drives behavior on the basis of need satisfaction, whether that need be personal, social, biological, or learned. The greatest need elicits the greatest response to meet that need, but religious thinking unconsciously prioritizes needs in relation to the ego. Mystical thinking does not limit the creation of meaning to egocentric values and so makes it possible for our species to create whatever meanings work best to satisfy the most needs of the most people involved in a given situation.

Consider the example of human sexuality. Because sexual behavior directly affects the process of evolution, all cultures place very strict controls on sexual activity. In our traditional Christian culture, for example, sexual behavior is only allowed within the context of a heterosexual, monogamous relationship. This limitation denies a normal, healthy sex life to millions of Americans, such as divorced individuals, gays, and widows or widowers. Furthermore, all religions condemn prostitution, which is patently irrational. This massive denial of perfectly legitimate human need is a stark reminder that cultures are not devoted to individual happiness, but first and foremost, to imposing the instinctual norms of that particular reproductive community on each individual.

X. Christian Marriage

Cultural anthropology established long ago that over the course of human history the definition of both marriage and family were determined by the environment of each particular reproductive community. Since cultures evolved as the collective adaptation of the community to its environment, there have been a variety of cultural definitions. Because most environments have been characterized by scarcity for most of our history and children can make real contributions to the survival of the family, natural selection—and therefore traditional cultures—promote high birth rates. As a result, we find many cultures in our past and present that favor unlimited pregnancies and multiple wives per family—since men are capable of fathering many more children in nine months than any one woman could bring to term. Here again, we see cultural evolution following biological evolution, as exemplified in the well-known theory of sexual dimorphism.[25]

United States culture began as a direct offshoot of the Judeo-Christian culture of Europe, in which monogamy was the ideal definition of marriage, even though it seems to have been rarely followed by the rich and powerful. Today, most objective observers of American culture would agree that the institution of marriage is in serious trouble: the divorce rate and the rapid increase in the number of unwed mothers and single-parent families being primary indicators. I would suggest that the essential problem with traditional marriage is that it is an example of our instinctual culture, rather than the mystical teachings of the founder of Christianity. Our culture presents marriage as a primary source of emotional gratification, which is simply the instinctual definition of happiness. But that definition, combined with the requirement of monogamy, reveals the same cultural bias toward the well-being and stability of the reproductive community, not the emotional well-being of the marriage partners.

Here again, we see the same reliance on altricial programming to control behavior rather than allowing each individual to exercise her or his own personal judgment. We see this with regard to the idea of *impure* sexual thoughts. Because egocentric consciousness is just a modification of our original hominin instinctual consciousness, it relies upon enculturation, especially religion, as its primary means of controlling behavior. The result is a great deal of unnecessary stress and conflict within the minds of its followers. There is no rational reason why we could not create a culture that engages the full capabilities of its members to think for themselves and learn from their own experiences. In terms of monogamy, there is no reason why married partners cannot share their experiences of sexual attraction to others and arrive at a mutually acceptable policy for dealing with those desires.

Such spiritual individualism is a primary achievement of the mystical tradition within the Judeo-Christian tradition, yet our traditional ideals about marriage remain instinctual. Many contemporary Americans entering a traditional marriage today expect it to be their primary source of emotional support and happiness, so they are doomed to frustration as they attempt to live out that ideal. The most common conflict in the early years of such a marriage revolve around the instinct of jealousy. Each partner expects the other to have no sexual or emotional attachments outside of the marriage, which is simply the manifestation of the ego's desire to control whatever is important to it, i.e., jealousy. But such a requirement often conflicts with the natural, healthy desires of both partners once the novelty—and hormones—of the marriage relationship wear off. And this inherent conflict is aggravated by our own culture, which so highly values personal freedom and self-determination. Our modern, secular culture, with all of its conflicting values, is the major reason why so many American marriages end in frustration and failure.

No one who has read the parables of Jesus, the farewell discourses in John's Gospel, or Paul's first letter to his congregation in Corinth could possibly think that jealousy, control, or judgmentalness are anything but indicators that a marriage (or any other relationship) is not Christian.

The only form of marriage that is compatible with individualism, and the mystical tradition from which it came, is one in which the partners define their relationship as an end in itself. Christian marriage cannot include any form of control, judgmentalness, or any other negative meanings. Consider the meaning of the concept of trust in marriage. According to egocentric consciousness, marital trust means trusting that one's spouse would never do anything that violated one's *own* values. But in that definition of the term, trust simply becomes a subtle form of spousal control. Mystical Christian trust means that each spouse trusts that whatever the other does must have a positive value for the relationship. In which case, the spouse would eagerly want to learn what that positive meaning is. Of course, neither spouse is obliged to agree with the values of the other, but each must make a good faith effort to understand the positive value of the other. If, after a loving dialogue, they cannot agree on a shared set of values, then they should dissolve the marriage. The only reason religion defines marriage as lifelong is because of evolution's 'need' for adequate child reading, which is an entirely separate issue.

Given this understanding of marriage, it is clear that only two people who have achieved mystical consciousness would be able to maintain a truly Christian marriage. For anyone else, marriage can serve as an excellent challenge to develop one's own spiritual potential, in which the marriage vows would simply be a solemn promise to give up any desire to control or morally judge one's spouse. Obviously, in such a marriage, both partners would be free to engage in whatever kind of relationship with anyone else, so long as that relationship also incorporated the same mystical values as the marriage. The full potential of human love and the instinctual need for control, manifested as judgmentalness, are mutually exclusive.

Another example of the instinctual bias of religion is its teaching about the distribution of power within the family structure. Traditional Christian marriage promotes a hierarchical structure with a standard chain of command, headed by the husband/father, who is morally responsible to follow, and also enforce, traditional Christian values. Yet the development of individualism as a cultural value is, I believe, the greatest achievement of Western culture. Many marriages would be far more successful if the partners had worked out their differences in advance regarding when and under what circumstances control should be exercised by each one of them.

XI. THE EVOLUTION OF CHRISTIANITY

Just as scientific psychology has to free itself from its religious presuppositions, beginning with the work of Herman von Helmholtz, so Rudolph Bultmann began a revolution in Christian theology that culminated, I believe, in the seminal work of John Dominic Crossan, the cofounder of the Jesus Seminar. According to this "radical" reinterpretation of the New Testament, Jesus never claimed divinity or any other form of supernatural existence or knowledge. He taught nothing about life after death or any kind of final judgment; nor did he claim the existence of a heaven or hell, the end of the world, or a god who controlled human history. He did teach that the Kingdom of Heaven (i.e., a fully human community that can be created here and now) was a real psychological possibility, but can only be achieved if we learn to create meaning using present-centered consciousness. I believe that Jesus was suggesting that if we changed from our egocentric form of consciousness to the mystical consciousness that he experienced, which I define as scientific spirituality, we would thereby bring about a new heaven and a new earth, beginning now. In other words, if we practiced this fully human form of consciousness, we would love ourselves and others as Jesus loved everyone and that would transform the world that we would eventually create over many generations. This radical change in the way we create meaning is what Jesus was referring to when he used the term "to be born again" or "*metanoia*" in the original Koine Greek of the New Testament.

We have already seen that the teachings of all the great mystics cannot be communicated by language because they refer to a fundamentally different form of consciousness. Only those who have already had some direct experience of this non-egocentric consciousness can understand the full meaning of teachings about it. Consequently, the mysticism of the founders of all the world's great religions were inevitably misinterpreted by the religious institutions that were created by their well meaning followers. The early Christian community, operating on the basis of egocentric consciousness, and wanting to both understand and spread the teachings of Jesus beyond the Jewish community, drew upon the most respected intellectual tradition of that time in the Roman empire: Neo-Platonism.

Plato was probably a mystic, but his followers certainly were not. So Neo-Platonism—and thus institutional Christianity, which was deeply influenced by it—is just another instinctual culture, i.e., an egocentric value system and the spiritual materialism it produces, just as all religions have always been. I believe Jesus was the personification of mysticism, so he understood that all symbols are created, not discovered or revealed. His use of the term *metanoia* is the essence of his teaching. The normal meaning of this Koine Greek word at that time was "to turn around, or reverse direction." Institutional Christianity has always interpreted this symbol to mean repentance, i.e., to repent for one's sins and to love and follow Jesus. Psychologically, this misinterpretation has come to mean that if we just love Jesus enough our sins will be forgiven and to we will get into Heaven ("the Kingdom of God") when we die. In practice, Christian tradition has turned Christianity into a kind of personality cult, rather than a devoted attempt to teach people to live out the mystical values that Jesus himself taught.

The true meaning of this term, I believe, can be found repeated in various forms throughout the New Testament. For example, The Sermon on the Mount, the parables of reversal, such as the Good Samaritan, the Final Discourses in John, Jesus' teaching to Nicodemus about spiritual rebirth, Paul's teachings on the nature of the Kingdom of God, are all proclaiming the same basic idea of *metanoia* as Jesus understood it. To be a Christian means to live one's life based on unconditional acceptance of other people. But this way of life requires a radically different form of consciousness that is not a product of biological evolution—which egocentric consciousness is, as we have seen.

The Kingdom of God that Jesus envisioned does not exist in space and time. It is simply any human community based on mystical consciousness. It must be created and believed in by each individual member. It can only exist as an expression of mystical spirituality, not religion. The United States Constitution (and similar non-instinctual social movements, like public education and the abolition of slavery), for example, includes some mystical theology, not politics (which is always egocentric). Metanoia means choosing the full creative potential of the individual and society over such ego gratification as inflicting fear and/or punishment on anyone who threatens one's own ego. This is the true spiritual path, and every child begins on that path. It is culture that teaches us all to be egocentric, instead. Enculturation into egocentric consciousness is the original sin.

For Jesus, the spiritual life meant giving up our natural predisposition to perceive our needs as having priority over those of others, a defining characteristic of egocentric consciousness. Being born again requires giving up all forms of motivation based on egocentric fear and in its place creating motivation based on all needs, including our own needs but on an equal footing with those of others. Mystical consciousness perceives need and responds accordingly, regardless of whose need it may be. That is the true spiritual path, which psychology refers to as self-actualization and which I believe can result in creating the kingdom of heaven in the future of our species.

I believe this is what Jesus was trying to communicate when he spoke at what is commonly known as the "Last Supper." He was telling his followers a psychological parable when he asked them to believe that bread and wine could be considered equal to his body and blood. The meaning of that parable was that we humans can create any meaning out of any experience, so we should use this ability to create positive meanings, symbols, and rituals that promote human happiness for all the members of our species.

Another way of teaching this same spiritual truth using scientific concepts is to tell everyone to live based on the assumption that we are all doing our best to satisfy our own needs—which is the ultimate motivation of every life form on earth. Consider for a moment a situation in which a policeman just gave you a speeding ticket or your boss just fired you. You can choose to respond to these stimuli by feeling angry and frustrated. Or you can choose to believe that those people were simply doing the best they could under those circumstances. As scientific psychology has shown, being angry and critical of others will have no effect on them, but it will do harm to you because every time you stimulate your anger circuits, you simply make them stronger, thus increasing the unhealthy influence of anger and stress in your own life. You serve your own best interests, and those of others, by creating positive feelings out of all such negative encounters. I suggest that if every member of our community created such positive meanings, we could work together to solve the problems in our world that gave rise to those potentially negative situations in the first place. This is the essential teaching of all the great mystics—as well as the real meaning of the words Jesus spoke at the Last Supper—and the key to the next stage of human evolution. We will only succeed in creating a fully human world if we choose to create only positive meaning out of all our experiences. Generating negative affect is not a necessary part of human life. In fact, it is an intrinsically unhealthy choice.

I would be remiss if I did not discuss those people whose needs are intrinsically unhealthy, such as serial murderers, in relation to present-centered consciousness. Such individuals must, of course, be removed from society and then helped to regain a healthy mental state, if possible, and only then reintegrated into society. It is important to note, however, that such severely ill people are not the cause of the enormous problems and dangers that beset our world. The conflicts that threaten the future of our species are the result of perfectly normal people who are, in fact, doing the best they can. The essence of the problem is not the activities of "bad" people or the vast majority of the mentally ill. It is our normal, instinctual way of creating meaning that is the cause of so much that is wrong with the human condition today. For example, consider America's last three wars: Vietnam, Iraq, and Afghanistan. Most Americans supported each one of those wars when they began, as the best solution to very difficult problems, but we then grew to understand that all three were becoming ultimately self-defeating disasters. But violence is always an instinctual response, never a mystical one. It is these kinds of responses that threaten the future of our global village, not plots by evildoers or the work of damaged or defective individuals.

XII. Scientific Spirituality

Scientific psychology is moving ever closer to the discovery that present-centered consciousness is the optimal form of mental health. Carl Jung began this branch of psychology with his ideas on self-actualization and the transcendent self. Abraham Maslow, Carl Rogers and Mihaly Csikszentmihaly, to cite just a few examples, have made major contributions to develop this school of positive psychology which can now be found in any introduction to psychology college text. This tells us that scientific psychology is on the cusp of discovering that the mystics were right: present-centered consciousness is the optimal form of happiness.

We have seen that our present way of creating meaning out of experience is instinctual and past-centered because it creates meaning by processing synaptic patterns through synaptic pathways that were created in our childhood acculturation and encapsulated in the ego. But scientific spirituality, or mystical consciousness, which must be consciously learned, creates meaning by assuming the priority of present sensory patterns over past learning. Zen Buddhism, in particular, has developed this psychological understanding of mystical experience, and Western science is now advanced enough to begin to integrate that model into its own theoretical landscape.

The scientific method itself, in fact, is an example of this same spiritual methodology. To conduct a proper experiment, the investigator must assume a psychological framework in which the sensory stimulations created by the observation of the experimental data are not interpreted according to past learning but are accepted for themselves and their properties. This is what science means by the essential characteristic of objectivity: being intellectually and emotionally open to discovering a new meaning in a particular experience, as defined by the experiment itself. The scientific experiment is the institutionalization of the mystical way of creating meaning out of experience. It is a way of thinking that is considered unusual or specialized only because our normal way of creating meaning is to interpret our present in terms of what we already know.

What our culture considers normal consciousness includes a tendency to preconsciously defend our self-concept from stress or contradiction, as Freud's defense mechanisms demonstrate so well. So, normal egocentric consciousness by its very nature judges present experience and distorts it whenever possible to reduce stress, as Rogers points out in his theory of incongruence.[26] The scientific method requires us to disarm our defense mechanisms and accept our experimental experience as fully and completely as we can. And this is, I believe, exactly what the great mystics, such as the Buddha, Moses, Jesus, and Mohammad were trying to teach, though the only vocabulary available to them to describe this was from their religious tradition and was, as a result, both misleading and inadequate to capture their radical message.

Unlike the instinct for survival—which motivates all animals on the basis of fear or desire—mystical consciousness is based on the belief that all forms of fear and desire can be overcome as motivators and replaced by the development of a more integrated, transcendent, and comprehensive form of consciousness. Egocentric (i.e., religious) consciousness judges the present in terms of past learning (acculturation) and limits personal growth to the boundaries of the self-concept. Mystical consciousness, on the other hand, promotes open-ended, unlimited personal growth and development because it accepts present experience as an end in itself, rather than as a means to reinforce the self-concept. When full mysticism is achieved, it automatically provides the individual with whatever motivation is required to respond fully and completely to the present experience without prioritizing and without fearing the consequences.

Just as the first of the world's great religious traditions began in the East with Hinduism, so also the first of the great mystics emerged there also. Through a lifetime of spiritual trial and error, Siddhārtha Gautama discovered that the human mind is capable of creating any meaning out of any experience, so he chose to let go of fear and create only positive meanings, which is the path to full human consciousness (i.e., enlightenment). The great Western religions began with Judaism, which produced the first great Western mystic, Jesus, whose teachings were essentially the same as the Buddha: give up egocentric fears and rejoice in life for its own sake.

We have seen that the real evolutionary value of the religious mentality, whether East or West, is to create a stable, hierarchical culture on nonrelated individuals, and that is why it was selected for in the course of our prehistoric evolution. Religion is a mental and behavioral control mechanism. That is why it condemns compromise as a betrayal of God's will: if you believe you possess absolute truth, compromise is a form of the sin of disobedience. True mysticism exchanges this fear-driven, control-oriented consciousness for a developmental, growth-oriented consciousness because mysticism replaces fear with acceptance and replaces judgment with love. The mystic responds to experience without fear or judgment because she or he believes there is nothing in the universe to fear, including death. Religious consciousness, being egocentric, is driven by the fear of death and damnation, as well as the desire for eternal, egocentric happiness.

Across the last six hundred years, the spiritual values of mysticism have gradually permeated Western culture, driving many of the cultural movements we think of as separate historical developments. Major historical moments motivated by mystical influence include, for example, the rise of Renaissance humanism in the fifteenth century, the Reformation in the sixteenth century, the scientific revolution in the seventeenth century, the Enlightenment and the theory of democratic government in the eighteenth century, the Industrial (scientific) Revolution in the nineteenth century, and the recent advances in social justice, such as progressive income tax, social security, universal health care, and the various civil rights movements. These ideas were all products of mystical insights of particular individuals in particular historical circumstances. We now are presented with a contemporary Western culture that is a chaotic mixture of instinctual, religious consciousness and the relatively new and emergent spiritual consciousness. The history of civilization is essentially the product of the conflict between these two psychological forces: the social stability of instinctual consciousness versus the developmental individualism of spiritual consciousness.

XIII. Religion and Politics

The contemporary American state of party politics is simply a microcosm of the clash between the instinctual, egocentric consciousness of conservative politicians and the emerging spiritual consciousness of the progressive community. As we have seen, this not a question of one group being right and the other wrong. Both factions are expressing real aspects of our shared human nature, and both are doing the best they can, given the way they create meaning. The problem is that the human mind is not a homogenous product of an integrated and comprehensive CNS. As I have tried to demonstrate, human nature is a work in progress, subject to the blind and irrational force of evolution. Science, in the form of psychology, is just now beginning to develop a theoretical model of the salient differences between our two basic ways of creating meaning out of experience. Michael Shermer has reviewed current academic studies on the psychological differences between political liberals and conservatives, and he has arrived at the following conclusion:

> In other words, liberals question authority, celebrate diversity, and often flaunt faith and tradition in order to care for the weak and oppressed. They want change and justice even at the risk of political and economic chaos. By contrast, conservatives emphasize institutions and traditions, faith and family, and nation and creed. They want order even at the cost of those at the bottom falling through the cracks.[27]

I interpret these differences as manifestations of the conflict between religious consciousness and spiritual consciousness. Natural selection programmed our species to value unchanging culture, tradition, and hierarchical social structures because these social values promoted our survival as hominin hunters and gathers. Commitment to the received values of ancestors, including culture, religion, and maintaining a stable social order, were critical for survival as long as we remained in our original African environment. In that context, the happiness of each individual member of the tribe was trivial in comparison to the survival of the reproductive community as a whole, which is the same principle we follow to this day when we send our young people to war. But leaving that original, evolutionary environment has brought about fundamental changes in our CNS, as we have seen, and those changes have expanded our human needs exponentially. The increasing awareness of this new potential has two dimensions: our need as individuals to develop our personal, unique potential, and our need as social animals to maintain positive relationships with other people.

When it comes to contemporary politics, it is important to note that religion evolved as the ultimate source of emotional enforcement for whatever values the local culture prescribed. However, because the United States Constitution requires the separation of church and state, the government cannot be an enforcer of any particular moral value system. The genius of the First Amendment is that it frees future generations of Americans from having to maintain immutable values, which could not always be, of course, rational adaptations to a constantly changing environment. Remaining blindly committed to the culture of the founding fathers would make us subject to the same fate as all past great nations: decline and fall. Fortunately, the First Amendment reflects the first law of evolution and recognizes the biological truth that in order to continue, life must adapt to the present environment or face extinction.

Clearly understanding the egocentric tendency to become addicted to power, the founding fathers also instituted the concept of separation of powers within the institution of government. However, they did not foresee another manifestation of this egocentric addiction in terms of political parties within government. I do not think that the idea of institutionalized political parties is even mentioned in the Constitution. But at this point in American political history, it is clear that our two traditional political parties, Democratic and Republican, are in fact more motivated to seek ever more power than to serve the people of this great country. The symptoms of this addiction are in the public domain: the gerrymandering of electoral districts, unlimited and unending campaigning, closed party primaries, and campaign finance reforms that are permeated with loopholes. In any real democracy, the people elect their representatives, but in the United States today, our representatives have the power largely to choose who can vote for them.

If the United States is to continue to lead the world as a model of democratic governance, as well as economic performance, the American people must take action to abolish these tools that both parties use to institutionalize their shared monopoly on power. Both parties want to keep the electorate focused on individual politicians and candidates, but that simply distracts us from the real problem, which is the power structure that both parties have carefully constructed over decades. Both the Occupy Wall Street movement and the Tea Party are excellent steps forward in raising our consciousness as to both the egocentric addiction to power and the corrupting role of money in politics.

XIV. THE PROBLEM OF INSTINCTUALLY BASED CONSCIOUSNESS

The key to making a smooth transition to the next form of consciousness is understanding that meaning exists only in the human mind and not in nature (i.e., all meanings are personal creations). Facts exist in reality, but the meaning of those facts exists only in our own mind. Our full human potential can only be realized when we decide to take responsibility for the meanings we create every day. Egocentric/religious consciousness was not selected for because it served the individual: it was selected for as an adaptation to our prehistoric environment. Thus, the ego is past oriented, hierarchical, and driven by the symbolized fears and desires of our hominin ancestors. But all those emotional values we share today are simply the product of our hominin instinctual needs as amplified by the ego itself. Our instincts, and the emotions they engender in us every day, have no validity beyond the environment in which they evolved at the beginning of our species, when we were just another hominin species migrating out of Africa.

The first essential evolutionary advance of our instinctual consciousness, emerging some one hundred thousand years ago, enabled us to adapt very rapidly to the radically new environments we encountered as we migrated out of Africa. This brings us to the conclusion that the human brain did not evolve in order to achieve rational thinking or absolute truth but rather to achieve membership in the reproductive group by means of social and cultural programmability—which is the ultimate form of animal adaptation to an environment marked by danger and scarcity of resources. Even though it is limited to a minimum unit of change of one generation, it was nonetheless a vast improvement over the purely biological rate of adaptation, which takes many generations to produce permanent cultural change. Thus, the human mind evolved for the purpose of being programmed by the group in such a way that the individual adult uses that programming not only to recreate learned social meanings but also to interact successfully within the reproductive group. Symbolization (i.e., connected synaptic patterns) is simply an efficient neurological process for storing, communicating, and learning from past experience. The purpose of our instinctually driven symbolic self-consciousness is to learn the socially accepted meanings that are essential to membership in the reproductive group and so shape our behavior accordingly.

XV. Conclusions

1. Learned Needs Function Like Instinctual Needs

I am proposing that our particular form of symbolic self-consciousness was selected for because it produces learned needs that function in our minds in essentially the same way as animal instincts do in other species. Once learned in childhood, these needs limit and shape behavior—much like genetically inherited instincts do in other primates. These culturally induced needs serve evolutionary values in two ways: 1) by ensuring that individuals will quickly respond to instinctually important stimuli with behaviors that have typically been successful in the past, and 2) by acting as models that transmit proven social behaviors, like language, to each new member of the reproductive community. The result is that this instinctual, culturally conditioned learning has always provided the meanings and motivation in daily life throughout human history. The essence of this evolutionary theory is that the human CNS is designed to be programmed in childhood, to live by those learned values throughout life, and to resist change in adult life unless such change is instinctively/egocentrically necessary.

2. The Social Function of Symbolic Consciousness

This new form of instinctual consciousness enabled early *Homo sapiens* to satisfy learned needs while maintaining social acceptability, thus making possible a much more complex, interdependent social system, built on social reciprocity and eventually, the specialization of labor. However, the price of this radically new form of adaptation was, and still is, a very limited form of consciousness, because it is emotionally bound by cultural programming that occurs before the individual is capable of evaluating the full implications or consequences of those learned needs, attitudes, and values. As a result of this very limited developmental process, our socially acquired self-concept becomes the ultimate context out of which we create meaning and so our adult lives tend to be simply extensions of that childhood programming.

3. Intrinsically Judgmental Consciousness

This form of self-consciousness made the preconscious modification of direct experience a mental necessity because that cognitive function is the primary means of shaping individual behavior to conform to the cultural values of the reproductive group. Thus, self-consciousness and self-judgment are implanted in the child as the most basic requirement, and the lowest common denominator, for group membership. Only by being programmed with this form of consciousness will the individual be accepted as a member of the community. The ancient religious rite of baptism, for example, is simply the formal, religious expression of this type of instinctual social processing. As long as our behavior conforms to established social standards, we will be acceptable into our social group, and, of course, that membership is crucial to our own survival. Perhaps it was this ability to combine learned needs with instinctual needs that made our social activities, such as hunting and intertribal warfare, intrinsically superior to those of the other hominin species, which is why we alone have, so far, escaped extinction. We most probably won the competition with Neanderthal, for example, for scarce resources by means of our superior verbally based social organization, which allowed us to annihilate and possibly even eat our hominin competitors.

4. Self-Consciousness Began as a Social Control Mechanism

The evolutionary breakthrough that made this advanced form of social organization possible was instinctual self-consciousness, and religious, or metaphysical, thinking is the essence of this form of self-consciousness because it programs us to create meaning based on our socially imposed self-concept. Ever since then, when we learn self-consciousness, we are learning to perceive ourselves as we are perceived by those who are important to us. Consequently, this form of consciousness is intrinsically social and includes an instinctual need to enforce its values on us and all other individuals. Thus, this form of consciousness is inherently judgmental. It makes us judge ourselves to see if we are socially acceptable to "ourselves"—but that really means acceptable in terms of the values of the important people in our childhood.

As Cooley discovered one hundred years ago, in his looking-glass theory, self-perception is by its very nature a learned, social activity.[28] This function is now widely accepted in psychology and is even beginning to appear in philosophy. In Jacque Lacan's theory of the dialectic of recognition, for example, he proposes that we get knowledge of what we are from how others respond to us. In other words, we each learned to think of ourselves not in terms of our own direct experience of ourselves but in terms of how our parents and others important to us perceived us in childhood. This is simply one more example of the fundamentally social nature of symbolic self-consciousness and its essential role of fitting each individual into the appropriate social system. Our own adult self-concept is not our creation but was implanted in us by our early social context. It is society's way of conditioning us to conform to its norms and values, not to our own unique combination of biological characteristics and developmental influences. As I have argued, we evolved to think this way because this form of consciousness maximizes the probability that we will be successful in terms of genetic reproduction within our cultural environment.

A pertinent example of the control function of egocentric consciousness can be seen in the structure of organizations in a civilized environment. All human organizations began as collective responses to some human need. Education, for example, began as an extension of acculturation that applied our instinctual programming to the specific needs of civilized societies, such as writing, reading, and understanding morality. Slowly, individuals came together for the purpose of establishing and improving moral education as a social service. Then these organizations of individuals developed into educational institutions with their own hierarchy and organizational culture;

however, once they became established within an egocentric society, the relationship of the individual to these organizations changed dramatically.

In the beginning of any new social institution, there are just separate groups of people who decide to work together to better serve the needs of their reproductive community. But when such groups grow large enough to become part of the fabric of society, they become institutionalized. Once that establishment occurs, the institution acquires the power to meet the needs of its own members and so it can exert control over them. Consequently, individual members begin to perceive membership in that institution as an end in itself. This happens because egocentric consciousness, being inherently social, is addicted to group membership and to increasing one's status within that group. The result is that organizations that began for the purpose of providing for some need in the community end up imposing needs on their own members and the community at large. Social psychology long ago established the enormous power of social organizations to control individual members. The classic examples are Stanley Milgram's famous studies at Yale of how easily individuals can be controlled by authority figures[29]; and more recently, Phillip Zimbardo's work at Stanford University on the power of even voluntarily established social roles to override the individual's moral values and even common sense.[30]

The history of religion is the very prototype of this sociological process. Organized religion began to meet the individual's emotional need for some sense of control over the environment and became a source of community support. But as religion became institutionalized, it slowly began to put requirements and controls on its members as the price of membership. Then it developed a hierarchy of priests, some of whom devoted themselves to further their own emotional needs within that hierarchy, rather than simply meeting the needs of the membership. In this way, the institution eventually becomes an end in itself, rather than a means to serving the needs of the people who make it up and whom it serves.

This same process applies to all socially established organizations, such as companies, financial institutions, health-care providers, political parties, and even governments. When schools, for example, become socially valued institutions, they put all types of restrictions and requirements on the students they originally just wanted to serve. In addition, various qualifications, standards, and hierarchies serve as mechanisms for controlling members. In this way, the teacher is as motivated to meet the career requirements of the institution as he or she is to meet students' needs. Because we are a social species, we are addicted to membership in groups and want to ascend the organizational hierarchy of those organizations. As a result, our lives are deeply influenced by the organizations we join, even when that influence is not in our own best interest. The recent sexual abuse scandal in the Pennsylvania State University football organization is another dramatic example of this phenomenon.

This process is especially evident in our current political parties. We may even have reached the point in which the party not in power is so motivated to regain power that they are willing to jeopardize the whole American political system and even the economy simply to ensure that the opposition party will be defeated. So it is that party politics, originally founded to serve the needs of the American people, have arrived at the point where they seriously consider sacrificing the common weal in order to advance their own power over the people. All in the name, of course, of "traditional values," which is the hallmark of religious consciousness. This constant conflict between the needs of the individual ego and the needs of the reproductive community is inherent within our instinctual/egocentric consciousness. The best solution to this problem is to take control of consciousness, as a natural resource, and design it scientifically to align the needs of the individual with the needs of the whole human species, not just the cultural group.

5. Our Self-Concept Is Never Our True Self

Our real self is simply our unique synthesis of genetic characteristics and our individual developmental history, but knowledge of that specific mix is practically impossible to acquire in childhood. Instead of accurate self-knowledge, instinctual consciousness imposes its socially derived self-concept on us at the beginning of our personality development, before we are capable of questioning whether it is accurate or even healthy. This universal process of human mind development demonstrates that the self-concept does not exist for the good of the individual but for the achievement of evolutionary goals. Here is the ultimate implication of the "selfish gene" idea that Richard Dawkins made famous.[31] The real self can only develop once we have an understanding of the evolutionary function of our own self-concept and its enormous influence on all of our subsequent experience. Only then can we understand that the meanings we have always created out of our experience are not our own but have been indirectly imposed upon us along with our self-concept, which is the preconscious context out of which all meaning is created.

In a similar way, the evolutionary function of the family has always been to instill and reinforce the instinctual values that are the foundation of all cultures. In other words, the preconscious role of the self-concept is the evolutionary mechanism by which human communities shape and control the behavior of their members. A consciousness built upon evolutionary values and self-judgment is the foundation of our present stage of evolution. Thus, the primary function of this form of consciousness is not to serve the well-being of the individual but to ensure the highest probability of the survival and reproduction of the gene pool, as Dawkins has argued so well.

Here we come face-to-face with the human predicament. We are a combination of two conflicting sets of needs: egocentric and social. Our instinctually driven developmental framework forms the foundation of the personality and so provides instinctual motivation for socially approved behavior. Every child is driven by instinct to acquire language and the symbolic consciousness that it requires because of an instinctual need for acceptance by the cultural community. Contemporary social science is just now bringing this inherent conflict between our egocentric and social needs into focus, but the most logical solution to this predicament is to rationally integrate the two into a prioritized value system. Such an integration would then consciously determine the meanings we create out of experience and would be the foundation of the next stage in the evolution of consciousness.

Instinctual consciousness does not value cognitive and emotive integration because it is driven only by whatever its lowest unmet need is at the given moment—as Maslow explained in his famous hierarchy of needs.[32] This inherent conflict between these value systems, our present instinctual system and our desire to become a fully integrated personality, now threatens the economic success and social progress that has been a hallmark of American culture. The majority of Americans continue to be raised in traditional Christian families and communities, which requires them to utilize egocentric consciousness in the service of the community's comprehensive social demands and expectations.

We have already seen that for evolutionary reasons, this form of consciousness is very resistant to change. Consequently, if Americans are not educated in the higher needs of their own nature and how to integrate those needs, they will, by virtue of de Tocqueville's tyranny of the majority, become an insurmountable obstacle to their own spiritual development and happiness and the continued social and spiritual evolution of American society. Without this scientific understanding of spirituality, American culture will self-destruct, resulting in the same decline and fall that has marked all previous great civilizations. However, if the majority comes to realize that egocentric meanings are not ultimate values, not even fully human values, then American culture will continue to lead the world in both social progress and individualism.

The best way to develop psychological potential, as we have seen, is to replace religious consciousness with spiritual consciousness, in the scientific spirit of such thinkers as Jung, James, Rogers, Maslow, and, most recently, E. O. Wilson. Religious consciousness represents the past of human evolution, while "mystical" spirituality represents the best possible future. Spirituality is about love, or "unconditional positive regard" to use Rogers's classic phrase, which is inherently social. One of its hallmarks is a willingness to agree to disagree and then use the scientific method to determine the best resolution of the conflict for all involved. Acceptance is vastly more important than agreement, unless your goal is to defend your own ego, of course. Spirituality is not about truth, control, or salvation, but about unlimited relationships and self-actualization. This means that the individual can only achieve self-actualization through healthy, non-judgmental relationships with other individuals. It also means, however, that mysticism cannot spread through the population until we replace our present, instinctual culture of control with a radically new culture of personal growth and development. Moreover, I believe that failing to make this transition in the near future will drive us toward self-defeating conflict on a national scale.

We tend to think of Western individualism as simply another variation in the long history of cultural evolution. However, I suggest that it is far more than that. It can be viewed as one of the first instances of "anticulture" in the history of evolution. Because individualism sprang out of rebellion against religion about one thousand years ago in Britain[33] and then spread to the rejection of every external locus of control, it represents the first social movement in history based on critical thinking and the rejection of traditional ways of thinking. I propose that the science of psychology must now make a commitment to studying consciousness as our ultimate natural resource, or else we will remain mired in the limitations of egocentric consciousness to our own detriment.

Now that cognitive science has arrived at a rudimentary understanding of the relationship between the biological activities of the CNS and the contents of consciousness, it would be irresponsible not to develop this new scientific frontier. Most people believe that their particular form of consciousness is inherent in our human nature and so it is the only normal form of consciousness. However, once we realize that consciousness is simply another learned manifestation of the evolutionary principle of adaptation, like the locking knee and the opposable thumb, we are led to the conclusion that "normal" consciousness is just an evolutionary adaptation to serve the goals of survival and reproduction, not an end in itself. So this consciousness is only as useful as the needs it serves, and those needs must now expand beyond the basic primate needs of sex and survival.

A new book by Nassir Ghaemi, *A First Rate Madness*,[34] is the first scientific proposal I have encountered that suggests that the value of any form of consciousness depends upon the environment in which it is functioning and thus should not be a cultural standard that defines the ideal form of human consciousness. In his introduction, Ghaemi states that the theme of the book is "The best crisis leaders are either mentally ill or mentally abnormal; the worst crisis leaders are mentally healthy."[35] This proposal may seem shocking because it violates our cultural bias about the transcendent nature of self-consciousness, but that kind of objectivity is the only scientific way to approach the study of consciousness.

In terms of my own theory, I would suggest that one of the most commonly accepted, yet unhealthy, characteristics of Western cultural consciousness is the belief that it is both necessary and healthy for the individual to inhibit the normal flow of consciousness. This belief is in keeping with the structure of egocentric consciousness (and thus religious thinking) that the ego is in control of the brain, when in fact the truth is precisely the opposite. Christian traditional teaching instructs us to impose its values throughout *every* stage of our own consciousness, even when it is just beginning to process sensory stimuli. We are taught, for example, that if we have what this tradition calls "impure sexual thoughts," we should immediately repress them—as seen in the teaching that if a man simply lusts after a woman in his heart, he has already committed a sin. But such a basic interruption of the normal process of synaptic processing can only result in intrapsychic conflict, which, from a scientific perspective, can only be unhealthy (i.e., neurotic).

Such a conscious act of mental repression requires that some circuits of the brain act in conflict with other circuits, thereby creating conflicting pathways within the neocortex itself. Scientific spirituality would teach that actual behavior (including verbal) is the currency of evolution and therefore is the province of morality, not the natural inclinations of our instinctual hominin nature. Therefore, it is perfectly normal for us to think of all the responses we may have to any given stimulus and only afterward decide on which response to manifest in our behavior. Morality only applies to our choice of which behavioral response we act upon. In fact, inhibiting the very process of decision making is itself abnormal and unhealthy and if engaged in repeatedly could easily lead to psychological damage (Hebb's rule). Just as we now realize that female circumcision is unhealthy, no matter how much any religious tradition may promote it, so also voluntarily and constantly inducing intrapsychic conflict upon ourselves is equally unhealthy and thus immoral.

Another serious mistake in traditional Christianity that is revealed by the evolutionary understanding of consciousness is the theological belief in revealed, absolute truth. No religion, or any other human activity, can bestow absolute truth upon its members because all knowledge is inherently subjective. Furthermore, a primary conclusion of my scientific model of the mind is that the CNS has the ability to create any meaning out of any experience, but no meaning can ever be absolute. Meaning does not exist in nature, only in the mind, because it is a product of the mind. Neither science nor religion can reveal absolute truth because all knowledge is relative to 1) the input provided by the environment, 2) the structure of the self-concept, and 3) the needs of the CNS at that moment. The very idea of absolute truth is an oxymoron, as is the concept of absolute freedom, both of which are theological doctrines that religion uses to justify and enforce its moral code. The only reason these contradictions are not obvious to everyone is because of the tremendous power of acculturation to bias our thought processes preconsciously.

I have tried to show in this book that ordinary consciousness, as we experience it every day, is just one form of consciousness, which itself is just an instinctual product of an evolutionary process that emerged along with grammatical language. In combination with our hominin consciousness, language produced self-consciousness and our capacity for abstract, symbolic thinking, but such thinking is still biased by its instinctual, preconscious processes. Religion is the social institution that evolved specifically to transmit adaptive behaviors to each new generation by means of acculturating this form of consciousness through such values as self-sacrifice and delayed gratification. But these are simply instinctual values selected for by evolution to promote a stable social order and increase the probability of survival and reproduction. This means that human thinking is naturally biased in favor of instinctual values, which makes instinct the ultimate source of all human motivation, including religious motivation. It is this instinctual motivation that has caused so much of the suffering and self-defeating behaviors that have plagued the history of civilization.

I have attempted to show that a variant form of consciousness, traditionally called mysticism, developed accidentally in a very few individuals and has had a gradual but profound influence on human history. The difference between instinctual and mystical consciousness is that instinctual consciousness creates meaning out of the present by judging it according to past learning and present needs, while mystical consciousness creates meaning by accepting present experience as an end in itself and then consciously applies past learning to create meaning out of the present. Unlike normal people, mystics do not preconsciously judge experience but instead accept it unconditionally, as it is experienced. Only after such unconditional acceptance of the present does the mystic create meaning and decide how to respond to it. We also see this psychological difference clearly in the scientific method, which is simply a recent application of mystical consciousness, because it requires us to accept all valid experimental outcomes, even when they contradict our understanding of reality (as in the case of quantum theory as applied to subatomic particles, for example).

Religion is the evolutionary product of instinctual consciousness. Its essence is the belief in a hierarchy that is ruled by a supremely powerful and omniscient judge. The goal of religion is to be rewarded by this imaginary supreme being for one's personal obedience to its authority. Thus, personal salvation is the ultimate value in any religion, which reveals its motivation is the instinct of egocentric survival. Scientific spirituality, or mysticism, is not instinctual or egocentric because it gives equal importance to all present needs, whether personal or those of others. It is simply another way, a noninstinctual way, of creating meaning out of experience that is only possible because it is an evolutionary by-product of self-consciousness. The goal of spiritual, or mystical, consciousness is simply to fully accept each and every personal experience for its own sake, not as a means to satisfy some egocentric need and not to be judged by any metaphysical priorities or values. In mystical/scientific consciousness, there is no such thing as absolute truth, only present experience. And every meaning is one's own creation.

The religious mind approaches each important experience with the metaphysical assumption it is a test from God that must be passed in order to gain salvation. Salvation is the learned, a priori need, rooted in the instinct for survival, which determines the meaning of every significant experience. The mystic, on the other hand, being free of instinctual or learned responses, is able to live each day to the fullest and not yearn for anything beyond the present experience. Religious consciousness constantly generates intrapsychic conflict, while mysticism generates an integrated, fully functioning mental state that can always create positive meaning out of the present moment. The mystic strives never to create negative emotional energy in any form.

Finally, I am proposing that our present form of consciousness, which is essentially instinctual, be replaced by present-centered consciousness in order to build a healthier and more communal social order. This social development would be the ultimate achievement of the individualism that has been evolving in Western culture for a thousand years. Once we extend our awareness into the preconscious process of the creation of meaning, we can pick and choose the most constructive and comprehensive meanings as our response to all experiences. This would be the ultimate achievement of individualism because it would free each mind from the socially imposed, preconscious limitations that evolution has made us all predisposed to accept as normative.

This possibility for transcending cultural limitations and instinctual conflicts is just one manifestation of the fact that consciousness is simply a natural resource. The liberation of the mind from its instinctual, preconscious limitations would instigate a profound advance in our history as a species—greater than the development of language or the rise of civilization. Societies that cultivate this natural resource will adapt best to the challenges of the future. Furthermore, present-centered consciousness will also enable the members of such a society to develop their personal cognitive and emotive abilities and creativity to their fullest capacity. Because consciousness is a natural resource, I find it useful to think of it in similar terms to electrical power generation. Everyone realizes that we must have electrical energy, but we must develop a technology for electricity generation that will not pollute our environment. So also we must develop a form of consciousness that will not generate the negative emotional responses that could destroy us.

The point of this book is to demonstrate that we already have such a capability and that it has been discovered by a few rare individuals across the centuries. Because of advances in the neurological and social sciences, we are just now beginning to realize the true salience of their discovery. Only recently has science begun to achieve a comprehensive theoretical model of the human mind, which enables us to begin understanding what the mystics already knew. By expanding our consciousness to take control of the "mystical" process, we can decide to create only positive meanings. So we can create a future in which hatred, misunderstanding, and self-criticism can be all but eradicated. Then, and only then, will we achieve a "new heaven and a new earth" that will be the foundation for a completely sustainable future for our species.

6. The American Experience

One of the most important issues we face right now is the fit between the environment and civilization. The success of any nation is determined by the ability of its culture to evolve along with the ever-changing environment, so that the people are always adapted to reality. When this balance exists, the full potential of the reproductive community and the individual can flourish. Because all cultures are inherently egocentric, however, they are quick to adopt environmental policies that reinforce egocentric values, but they are very resistant to changes that threaten the ego. American culture is especially vulnerable to this problem because we have given over our mass media to the profit motive. Because that motivation is overly instinctual, allowing it to determine the content of our cultural environment, which is what the mass media dominate, practically guarantees and reinforces the egocentric acculturation of our children. For example, as food and housing have become relatively cheap in the United States since the end of

World War II, American culture adapted by assigning positive meaning to larger meals and tax deductions proportional to the size and cost of homes. However, in spite of the fact that we now understand that overeating and over-mortgaging are not in the individual's best interest, our culture continues to consider elaborate, expensive meals and enormous homes a mark of success, not excess.

There has been much talk in the media lately about the theory of American exceptionalism, which, as I understand it, is the belief that the United States of America is significantly superior in its history and culture. It is a fact that this country was the first constitutional democracy, which is an enormous achievement, but I would suggest that the more important part is our constitutional separation of religious values from our legal system. All the great empires of history were governed by some form of divine-right monarchy, which taught that the ruling monarch was selected by God and thus was the ideal model whose values and laws must be followed by all members of that kingdom. This form of governance was probably favored by natural selection because it produced the most stable reproductive community most of the time for most of the people. Because the monarch personified God's will for all the people under his or her rule, the people had only to follow the royal religious values and legal decrees to be in God's favor and maintain a united body politic.

The United States introduced a radically different model of governance, no doubt influenced by the Protestant Reformation and contemporaneous French political thinking, by creating a legal system that allowed for individual freedom regarding religious and political values. In terms of the history of national governance, this was indeed exceptional. So much so, in fact, that when the Constitution became the law of the land, many Americans did not understand its full implications and did not follow it. The practice of slavery, for example, denied individual freedom to a large segment of the population, which led to the worst war in American history. Even today, American culture still harbors a significant degree of prejudice against its own minority citizens. These facts remind us of the tremendous resistance that all cultures have to changes that threaten the egocentrism of the majority, simply because the ego is driven by the deepest instincts of all: sex and survival.

It is the institutions, such as religious, educational, and economic organizations, that impose the core values of any culture on its members. When natural selection produces a new culture, those institutions closely reflect the natural and social environment to which that culture is an adaptation. But a problem always arises, as that environment inevitably changes, while social institutions inevitably resist all changes that are not egosyntonic. This is the proximate cause for the decline and fall of all the great civilizations of human history. We now understand that we are a social species, and so we naturally organize into hierarchal social structures. And the higher the individual climbs within those structures, the more emotionally committed he or she will become to maintaining the cultural status quo. The ultimate result of this social organization is that the culture becomes increasingly disjointed from its actual social context and as a result, its social institutions become increasingly oppressive, rather than constructive for the common good.

The American experiment of secular democracy certainly represents a fundamental advance in national governance. I would suggest, however, that it has only come about because of the influence of mystical values that are part of our Western "religious" tradition of individualism. The great mystics were the original individuals of history. But evolution has not stopped. Now we must advance to the next stage by integrating the eastern mystical tradition of present-centered consciousness into our Western individualism and so create the next evolutionary form of consciousness: scientific mysticism.

THE THREE STAGES OF
HUMAN EVOLUTION

Stage 1: Hominin Consciousness

Hominin consciousness is, like all primate consciousness, instinctual, but it is also more plastic than preceding species and so has significantly more learning capacity. Consequently, it is capable of some learned, emotional motivation, and it has some programmed culture, but minimal self-consciousness.

Stage 2: Linguistic Consciousness

The diaspora out of Africa created a highly adaptive stage in our evolution that increased plasticity enough to make grammar and syntax possible, which resulted in grammatical language and self- consciousness. This new, symbolic consciousness was a more successful adaptation to radically new environments, but this period of radical adaptation also resulted in CNS changes that produced intrinsic conflict between programmed self-consciousness and the social needs of the reproductive community. Furthermore, in this egocentric consciousness, meanings are preconsciously determined by social conditioning. Although egocentric consciousness made civilization possible and is practically universal in today's world, it is inherently unstable and socially unsustainable.

Stage 3: Fully Human Consciousness

Egocentric consciousness uses brain circuits to serve past learned needs or present instinctual needs. Satisfying present instinctual needs is perfectly healthy, but there can be very serious problems with satisfying past needs because the resulting behaviors are often out of sync with the present situation. Because of the power of acculturation, spiritual consciousness normally develops only as far as such mundane functions as paying attention and delaying gratification. This limitation problem arises because once the ego is formed it uses all CNS circuits to serve its instinctual needs.

Here is where the relationship between present and past becomes complicated. When we use the symbol "the present," we are ordinarily thinking of the objective or "real" present situation. But that use of the symbol is culturally biased by our "quasiscientific" way of thinking. The objective present does not exist in any human mind because, by definition, it would have to include not only every physical object in a given situation but also every state of mind of every person in that situation, including one's own, which is impossible. What we really mean when we speak of "the present" is our own perception of that situation, which could not possibly be a complete and objective understanding of that entire set of circumstances. In other words, when we talk about the present, we are referring to a myth of our popularized scientific culture, not scientific reality. It is scientifically impossible for any two human beings to perceive the same situation in exactly the same way, thus the concept of knowing any situation in a completely objective way is a human impossibility. Nevertheless, our culture teaches our ego to invoke this myth when it serves our own egocentric needs to do so.

The spiritual person understands that the only reality anyone can experience is one's own personal reality. Thus, spiritual consciousness means never invoking objectivity in an attempt to manipulate or judge another person. A scientific understanding of individualism requires us to realize that we can never judge another on the basis of our own understanding of reality because that reality is intrinsically biased and idiosyncratic (hence, Matthew 7:1–6).

True spirituality requires that we understand not only our own but also the other person's perception of reality, as best we can. If we do not have that knowledge, then we do not have a valid (i.e., spiritual) relationship with that person. Without that spiritual knowledge, our perception of the other is nothing but a projection of our own ego. The spiritual person understands that symbols must be used very carefully because they can so easily become an instrument of self-deception. Integration is the key to successfully understanding reality. Using this model, decision making is a time consuming, three stage process:

- Fully and completely follow through on your own initial emotional response to the stimulus, including all behavioral impulses, until the emotional energy is dissipated, no matter how long that takes.

- Act only on those behaviors that are expressions of the personal values you truly believe in.

- Learn from the consequences of your behavior and adjust your ideal self-concept accordingly. If we teach our children to habitually follow this process they will vastly increase their own happiness and improve the world at the same time.

Egocentric Consciousness Religion (Instinctual consciousness)	Spiritual Consciousness Present-centered (Learned consciousness)
• Religion is egocentric because it uses the ego as the preconscious context for the creation of meaning out of experience.	• Spirituality is present-centered because it uses present experience as the context for the creation of meaning out of experience.
• It is motivated by egocentric (instinctual) fears and desires.	• It is motivated by learned needs, leading to self-actualization.
• Its goal is conformity to socially determined values.	• Its goal is full personal growth and development.
• Its meaning is determined by learned theological and metaphysical presuppositions.	• Its meaning is created in the present and is thus the highest form of self-actualization.
• One's relationship to the imaginary god(s) is primary.	• One's relationship to self-development is primary.
• Divine revelation is absolute truth.	• Human nature is the ultimate truth.
• Experience is intrinsically filled with good and evil.	• Experience is intrinsically meaningless.
• Human nature is selfish.	• Human nature has unlimited potential.
• The ego is the ultimate reality that must be maintained at all times.	• The ego must be continuously outgrown by overcoming fears.
• Control over one's own experience is the ultimate goal.	• Accepting every experience with gratitude is the ultimate goal.

The Future of Consciousness

If we are to take control of our own future as a species, we must create a form of consciousness that is a rational adaptation to our ever-changing environment, which must automatically orient us toward a healthier mental life and a more developed human community. This new culture should be built on two principles: First, we have to change our psychological relationship to time by replacing past learning with present experience as the framework for creating meaning. Second, we must take responsibility for creating our own meanings. This is the essence of the teachings of all the great spiritual teachers of history and the key to the only fully human form of consciousness. In practice, this will take the form of a radically new culture that will instill the following values:

- I am the creator of all the meanings that I experience in life, and I am responsible to myself for their consequences.

- I can create any meaning out of any experience, but I should choose the one that is the best integration of my past learning and present experience.

- I am happiest when I create meanings that meet all of my present needs.

- My behavior is the most accurate expression of my needs, which is the only way I can discover what it is that I want.

- I create my most important relationships, and benefit the most from them, by accepting every relationship for what it is and learning from that relationship.

- Because we are a social species, intimacy (which is the unconditional acceptance of another) and its product, creativity, are the most rewarding expressions of human experience and the only means for achieving long-term happiness.

In conclusion, the basis of full human development is for each individual to integrate these presuppositions into the fiber of the preconscious mind, through acculturation, which is the primary means for achieving such deep, preconscious learning. Doing so will make these values the foundation of a fully developed consciousness and enable us to achieve our full uniqueness and make the greatest contribution to the human community.

Ω Ω Ω

NOTES

(Endnotes)

1. T. E. McNamara, Evolution, Culture and Consciousness (Dallas: University Press of America, 2004).
2. Ibid., 1.
3. E. O. Wilson, *The Social Conquest of Earth* (New York: Liveright Publishing, W. W. Norton, 2012).
4. While chimp sexual patterns are similar to our own, bonobos have evolved a radically more open and uninhibited form of sexuality. Cf. deWaal and Lanting, Bonobo: The Forgotten Ape. U. of California Press, 1997.
5. R. Davidson, *The Emotional Life of Your Brain* (New York: Hudson Street Press, 2012).
6. Hermann von Helmholtz (1821 – 1894) was the first major scientist to reject the Cartesian dualism of body and soul and replace it with the belief that the min is simply the product of the brain.
7. K. Armstrong, *The Great Transformation* (New York: Alfred A. Knopf, 2006), 391.
8. D. Kahneman, *Thinking Fast and Slow* (New York: Farrar, Straus and Girons, 2011).
9. M. Gazzaniga, *Who's in Charge?* (New York: Harper Collins, 2011), 112.
10. W. D. Hamilton, The genetical evolution of social behavior. Journal of Theoretical Biology, 7, 1-52. (1964)
11. M. Shermer, *The Believing Brain* (New York: Henry Holt & Co., 2011).

12. C. H. Cooley, *Human Nature and the Social Order* (New York: Scribner's, 1902); C. R. Rogers, *On Becoming a Person* (Boston: Houghton Mifflin, 1961).

13. E. O. Wilson, *Consilience: The Unity of Knowledge* (New York: Alfred A. Knopf, 1998).

14. M. Shermer, *The Believing Brain* (New York: Henry Holt & Co., 2011), 5.

15. G. M. Edelman and G. Tononi, *A Universe of Consciousness* (New York: Basic Books, 2000).

16. P. Boyer, *Religion Explained* (New York: Basic Books, 2001).

17. L. S. Vygotsky, *Mind in Society: The Development of Higher Mental Processes* (Cambridge: Harvard University Press, 1978).

18. D. Hebb, *The Organization of Behavior: A Neuropsychological Theory* (New York: Wiley & Sons, 1949).

19. M. Donald, *Origins of the Modern Mind* (Cambridge, MA: Harvard University Press, 1991).

20. R. A. Shweder, *Thinking through Cultures* (Cambridge: Harvard University Press, 1991).

21. A. Bandura, "Social Cognitive Theory," *Annual Review of Psychology* 52 (2001): 1–26.

22. E. D. Thiesen and J. R. Saffran, "Pattern Induction by Infant Language Learners," *Developmental Psychology* 39 (2003): 484–494.

23. J. Diamond, *Guns, Germs and Steel* (New York: W.W. Norton, 1997).

24. A. R. Fuller, *Psychology and Religion: Eight Points of View* (Lanham, MD: Littlefield Adams, 1994).

25. Many evolutionary biologists believe the relative difference in body size between males and females correlates with the typical number of sexual partners the average male of that species has over his lifetime. On that basis, the theory suggests that over the life of our species the typical made has had about 4 long term sex partners. Cf., M. Ridley, *Evolution*, 3rd ed. (Malden, Massachusetts: Blackwell, 2004); also, Martin Daly & Margo Wilson (1996). "Evolutionary psychology and marital conflict". In David M. Buss & Neil M. Malamuth. *Sex, Power, Conflict: Evolutionary and Feminist Perspectives*. Oxford University Press, 13.

26. Roger's theory proposes that egocentric consciousness is so powerful in shaping our perception of reality that it often distorts our perception of anything in our experience that conflicts with our self-concept. Rogers, Carl. *Client-centered Therapy: Its Current Practice, Implications and Theory*. London: Constable (1951).

27. M. Shermer, *The Believing Brain* (New York: Henry Holt & Co., 2011), p.240.

28. C. H. Cooley, *Human Nature and the Social Order* (New York: Scribner's, 1902).

29. S. Milgram, *Obedience to Authority: An Experimental View*. New York: Harper and Row (1974).

30. P. Zimbardo, *The Lucifer Effect: Understanding How Good People Turn Evil* New York: Random House (2007).

31. R. Dawkins, *The Selfish Gene* (New York: Oxford University Press, 1976).

32. The theory states that all human motivation is driven by needs. All needs exist in a hierarchy, with the most basic physiological needs at the bottom, ascending to safety needs, then attachment needs, then self-esteem needs and finally, at the top of the hierarchy, self-actualization. At any given time the individual is motivated by the lowest unmet need. Cf. Maslow's *Motivation and Personality*, New York; Harper and Row: 1954.

33. C. Morris, *The Discovery of the Individual 1050–1200* (Toronto: University of Toronto Press, 1972).

34. N. Ghaemi, *A First-Rate Madness* (New York: Penguin Press, 2011).

35. Ibid., 17.